W9-CPY-368

25 Jewels
in a
Silver Setting

Dr. Tom Wallace

Sword of the Lord Publishers

Post Office Box 1099 • Murfreesboro, Tennessee 37133

Copyright 1980 by
Sword of the Lord Publishers
ISBN-0-87398-836-1

Printed and Bound in the United States of America

Dedicated
to...

The many faithful and loyal staff members who have given themselves so unselfishly behind the scenes over these twenty-five years.

They have literally formed the platform from which I have stood and preached here and there and everywhere.

God bless them all.

Dr. Tom Wallace

Contents

Foreword

Dr. Tom Wallace, we salute you!

Twenty-five years of preaching with Bible in hand.

Twenty-five years of prayer and sermon preparation.

Twenty-five years of facing audiences—mostly frienc sometime indifferent, occasionally hostile.

Twenty-five years of inviting men to receive Christ.

Twenty-five years of welcoming repentant sinners int the fellowship of the saints.

Twenty-five years of baptizing converts—hundreds of them.

Twenty-five years of waiting on God.

Twenty-five years of seeking His perfect will for your life.

Twenty-five years of problems.

Twenty-five years of tears and heartaches.

Twenty-five years of working with God's people.

Twenty-five years of resting on His Divine promises.

Twenty-five years of proclaiming the good news of salvation.

Twenty-five years of fighting Satan.

Twenty-five years of rejoicing in the blessings of God.

Dr. Wallace, you have had all of this and more! I rejoice in your fruitful ministry and your faithfulness to the Saviour. I have heard you preach; I think I know your heart—you have one desire: to exalt Christ!

It is my prayer that God will give you twenty-five more years (if the Lord tarries His coming) to proclaim the unsearchable riches of Christ.

> Sincerely,
> Dr. Lee Roberson

Pastor Emeritus,
Highland Park Baptist Church
Chancellor,
Tennessee Temple University
Chattanooga, Tennessee

You hold in your hands twenty-five time-proven sermons from one of the great pulpiteers of our time. For forty-seven years, Dr. Tom Wallace has mounted pulpits across America with a smile on his face and a burden on his heart to see the lost saved and the lives of God's people changed. For forty-seven years, congregations have been captivated by his resonant voice as he delivered yet another "jewel" of a sermon that he had received from the throne room of Heaven.

For these last few years, I have had the privilege to be Dr. Wallace's pastor. Not only do I know him as a preacher and a writer, I know him as a church member and a soul winner. I have watched him be a godly husband and a father. His life is built into these messages.

As a pastor, I want to learn from pastors who have fought the battle and stayed the course. I am grateful that Dr. Wallace has allowed us to see part of his life in this book of sermons. May the Lord use these messages to transform us into the "jewel" that God would have us to be.

—Dr. Mike Norris

Pastor,
Franklin Road Baptist Church

Preface to the Second Edition

Old sermons never die, they just get reprinted. I am delighted that Dr. Shelton Smith and his editorial staff at the Sword of the Lord have decided to reprint *Twenty-Five Jewels in a Silver Setting.*

In the first edition I selected a message from each of the first twenty-five years of my ministry. I also chose twenty-five different themes from the Bible.

The messages for the most part are timeless enough to meet the reader's need at my fiftieth year of ministry also.

The theme of my ministry is still the same. I have two basic messages. The first is a message to sinners and deals with how they can go to Heaven when they die. The second is for the saint and deals with how to be happy in living for the Lord after salvation. These messages are all geared in one of these two directions.

It is my desire and prayer that many will be born into the family of God and that others will grow and develop in the grace of God through reading these messages.

Preface to the First Edition

The theme of these last twenty-five years has been

PREFACE

Heaven and happiness. One is a message for sinners, the other for saints. Jesus gave a summary of the Ten Commandments when He said that the first relates to God and the second relates to people. My relationship to God will get me to Heaven, while my relationship to people will bring me happiness.

The sermons in this book were preached with these two great thoughts in mind. It is my desire and prayer that many will be born into the family of God and that others will grow and develop in the grace of God through these messages.

The Velvet Alley

"There is a way which seemeth right unto a man, but the end thereof are the ways of death."—Prov. 4:12.

Sin is alluring to the eye, attractive to the flesh and very appealing to the carnal nature. Dr. R. G. Lee describes sin as a beautiful pansy bed with a deadly serpent hid beneath. In one of his sermons on sin, Dr. John R. Rice pictures sin as a beautiful red apple with a worm crawling inside. It is like an iceberg, with the great, jagged bulk hidden out of sight. It is a boomerang that always returns to its sender with consequences. Surely sin is a "velvet alley" with a beautiful entrance. But, once inside, it is filled with filth and ugliness.

It is not what it appears to be. It looks fine on the surface, but, oh, the tragedy and sorrow that is buried down inside! Adam and Eve discovered this awful street. Everything looked fine and Satan made it sound all right, but the human race has suffered ever since.

Achan learned too late that the price of sin was high. The gold, silver and goodly Babylonian garments certainly were attractive, but they were not worth being stoned to death. David went down the velvet alley when he saw and lusted after Bathsheba, but the fourfold payment that he suffered made him look back in regret. Ananias and Sapphira were lured into the alley by greed and lust and discovered how God feels about sin.

The prodigal son found that the attractive path led to a pig pen. Peter went out and wept bitterly after carelessly wandering into the tragic alley. Judas went out and hanged himself after realizing that he was too far down the dead-end street to turn back. Thirty pieces of silver looked good at first, but he threw them at the feet of the priests in disgust and shame. But then, it was too late!

The alcoholic has found that the cocktail and cold, thirst-quenching beer is not what it is cracked up to be. The fallen girl, unwed mother and the diseased, dying victim of venereal disease soon realizes that the alley is not velvet after all. The psalmist warned in Psalm 34:21, "Evil shall slay the wicked"; and in Psalm 140:11 we read, ". . .Evil shall hunt the violent man to overthrow him." Solomon said in Proverbs 8:36, "But he that sinneth against me wrongeth his own soul."

The velvet alley is the broad road that Jesus spoke about in the Sermon on the Mount. It leads to destruction. It is the road of sin. I want to look further into this thought under four headings: *I. THE DEFINITION OF SIN. II. THE DECEITFULNESS OF SIN. III. DEATH BY SIN. IV. DELIVERANCE FROM SIN.*

I. The Definition of Sin

The Bible says, "Whosoever committeth sin transgresseth also the law: for sin is the transgression of the law" (I John 3:4). To break God's law or to "miss the mark" is sin. The Ten Commandments were given to Moses by God as a standard. They are not intended to be a ladder by which to climb to Heaven, but a mirror through which we look over ourselves. Jesus taught that sin is committed by thought as well as deed. James states that to break one point of the law is to break it all.

Solomon defined sin as, "He that despiseth his neighbour sinneth" (Prov. 14:21). Paul explained that "whatsoever is not of faith is sin" (Rom. 14:23). James stated, "Therefore to him that knoweth to do good, and doeth it not, to him it is sin" (James 4:17). John wrote, "All unrighteousness is sin" (I John 5:17).

There are many different kinds of sin illustrated in the Bible. There is the secret sin—like Cain's; impulsive sin—like Esau's; coverered sin—like Joseph's brethren and Achan's; sin prompted by others—such as Ahab's; reluctant sin—like Samson's; sin under influence of alcohol—such as Belshazzar's; sin approved by authority—as in Judas' case; sins pleasing to the public—such as Pilate's sin; sin of ignorance—as pictured by the Jews in their rejection of the Messiah.

There are also sins of omission and sins of commission. That is, to "omit" or leave undone something that should be done and to go out and do something one should not do. In defining sin, D. L. Moody said, "The best way to show that a stick is crooked is to lay a straight one beside it." Romans 3:20 declares, "For by the law is the knowledge of sin."

II. Deceitfulness of Sin

The writer of Hebrews wrote, "But exhort one another daily, while it is called To day; lest any of you be hardened through the deceitfulness of sin" (Heb. 3:13).

Jeremiah stated that, "The heart is deceitful above all things, and desperately wicked" (Jer. 17:9), and the psalmist cried in Psalm 120:2, "Deliver my soul, O Lord, from lying lips, and from a deceitful tongue."

Sincere people are being deceived by false teachers and man-made religions. Many others are being led to believe that they can get by without God, the Bible, prayer and salvation. Jesus said, "Take heed that ye be not deceived. . ." (Luke 21:8). Paul warned, "Be not deceived; God is not mocked: for whatsoever a man soweth, that shall he also reap" (Gal. 6:7).

III. Death by Sin

"For the wages of sin is death. . ." (Rom. 6:23). "The soul that sinneth, it shall die. . ." (Ezek. 18:20). The sinner dies *in* sin, the Saviour died *for* sin, and the saint dies *to* sin. Death was promised to Adam and Eve, if they took of the tree. Spiritual death came the instant they sinned. Physical death followed. To those who do not accept the provision of eternal life by Christ, eternal death will come.

Eternal death is called "the second death." "And death and hell were cast into the lake of fire. This is the second death" (Rev. 20:14). The Bible speaks of a "sin unto death" that Christians can commit. This is to so ignore God's leading or speaking that He judges us in this life and removes the Christian out of this life. The velvet alley of sin always comes abruptly to a dead-end death.

IV. Deliverance From Sin

"For he hath made him to be sin for us, who knew no sin: that might be made the righteousness of God in him" (II Cor. 5:21). The penalty was hanging over our head, but payment and pardon was granted by Christ. The curse was passed to all, but the cure was found in Him. Judgment was for sure, but justification was revealed to us.

The story is told about an Indian who had seen the light. Trying to explain how to become a Christian, he made a circle of fire and placed a worm inside. The worm, running in every direction, soon became bewildered and exhausted. It was helpless. Just then, the Indian reached in and picked it up out of the fire.

This is exactly what Christ did for us. As the psalmist said, "He brought me up also out of an horrible pit, out of the miry clay, and set my feet upon a rock, and established my going" (Ps. 40:2).

To those who find yourselves deceived and suffering the misery of the effects of sin, may I urge you to come to Christ now and allow Him to put you on the main highway of abundant life.

Man on Fire

"And in hell he lift up his eyes, being in torments, and seeth Abraham afar off, and Lazarus in his bosom. And he cried and said, Father Abraham, have mercy on me, and send Lazarus, that he may dip the tip of his finger in water, and cool my tongue; for I am tormented in this flame."—Luke 16:23,24.

Recently I unfolded a metropolitan newspaper and glanced at the bold, two-inch headline, "MAN ON FIRE." It was an incident where a midwestern union official had been forced into a car, taken to the outskirts of town, drenched with gasoline or some highly flammable fluid, and set on fire. His picture was on the front of most every newspaper in the country. The newspaper described the painful misery of his charred body, and millions of people sympathized with the man. People are naturally sympathetic and their hearts go out to those who are victims of tragedy.

On December 1, 1958, the news of the Chicago school fire that burned 89 children and three nuns to death had raised the sympathy of the whole nation. Fire and tragedy are two words that go together. One New York newspaper called this particular fire, "A GLIMPSE OF HELL."

Not long ago, two ships collided somewhere out at sea off the New York coast. One of these ships was loaded with a million gallons of gasoline. The explosion and fire that followed resulted in many merchant seamen going down in what the newspaper called "AN UNQUENCHABLE FIERY GRAVE."

On March 18, 1937, some 294 school children and teachers died in a fire explosion in New London, Texas. On March 4, 1908, in the Collingswood school fire, in Cleveland, Ohio, 176 children perished. On November 28, 1942, as the cry, "FIRE," was screaming out at the Coconut Grove Night Club in Boston, several hundred people tried to rush through a revolving door at one time and 498 were burned to death. On December 30, 1903, the great fire disaster at the Iroquois Theater in Chicago brought tragedy by the loss of 575 lives in the fire.

In all these incidents people have cried out how horrible and awful it is to burn to death. I certainly agree that, in each of the 26 major fire disasters in which more than 50 people have been killed in the last 100 years, that this is a horrible, hysterical way to die. But I want to warn some of you that it is far more horrible to share the fate of the rich man of Luke 16, who cannot die and get it all over with, but must go on in the scorching, cracking flames of eternal Hell forever and forever. The circumstances and details of Hell are more horrible than all of the above-mentioned fire tragedies put together.

I. Why Preach on Hell?

Some have asked the reason for preaching on the horrible subject of Hell. I preach on Hell because I know that some of you who read this sermon will spend eternity there. So it is my duty to warn you to flee the wrath to come.

Hell is a terrible subject and the thought of burning flesh brings chills to me. Nothing is more painful or nauseating odor than burned flesh.

I was visiting a local hospital not long ago and stepped into a room where a man was in the bed, on his knees, with head down on his folded arms. I walked up to the man and said, "Sir, are you praying?" He answered, "No, Preacher, my back is burned so bad that this is the only position that gives me any relief." For several days I went there to see him and every time he was on his knees. I was reminded that in Hell relief won't come, even on the knees.

I have read how in past days men used to tie a man to a stick and build a fire under him. Then they would roll him over and over again, roasting him alive, like barbeque chicken, as a means of torture. How horrible! But still not as bad as Hell. In Foxe's *Book of Martyr's*, we have the account of many Christians being burned at the stake, and we read of great men, like John Knox, being tortured to death by fire.

The thoughts of death by fire are so horrible that no state in America will allow capital punishment on this basis. Some states allow that a criminal may be executed by the firing squad, some by the gas chamber, others by hanging and still others by the electric chair; but, no state law will allow burning a man to death. The people of the United States would rise up in rebellion if such a law were ever suggested.

Again, I preach on Hell because many people do not believe it is real. The modernist has discarded the old-fashioned doctrine of Hell on the basis of human reasoning. The Jehovah's Witnesses, Christian Scientists, Seventh-Day Adventists, Mormons and multitudes of others have thrown it out. The Roman Catholics have substituted a purgatory in place of it. Purgatory is not found anywhere in the Bible.

You, too, might find yourself doubting the reality of Hell, but I remind you that Jesus said there is a Hell. "And fear not them which kill the body, but are not able to kill the the soul: but rather fear him which is able to destroy both soul and body in hell" (Matt. 10:28). In our text, Jesus told the story of the rich man in Hell and again in Matthhew 13:49,50, He said, ". . . Angels shall come forth, and sever the wicked from among the just, And shall cast them into the furnace of fire: there shall be wailing and gnashing of teeth." In Matthew 25:30 we read, "And cast ye the unprofitable servant into outer darkness: there shall be weeping and gnashing of teeth." Jesus said in Matthew 25:41, ". . .Depart from me, ye cursed, into everlasting fire, prepared for the devil and his angels."

The Bible is our only source of information on this subject and it declares that there is a Hell. In Psalm 9:17 we read, "The wicked shall be turned into hell, and all the nations that forget God." Isaiah 14:15 states, "Yet thou shalt be brought down to hell, to the sides of the pit." We read in Revelation 20:15, "And whosoever was not found written in the book of life was cast into the lake of fire."

Great preachers of the past have declared a real Hell.

R. A. TORREY—"I claim to be a scholarly preacher and I believe the old-fashioned Bible doctrines regarding a Bible Hell."

D. L. MOODY—"The same Christ that tells of Heaven with all its glories, tells us of Hell with all its horrors."

H. W. BEECHER—"The thoughts of future punishment for sinners, which the Bible reveals, is enough to make an earthquake of terror in a man's soul."

T. DEWITT TALMAGE—"Not having intellect enough to fashion an eternity of my own, I must take the word of the Bible."

C. H. SPURGEON—"Hell, the saved one will not know. That wrath, he will not feel."

BILLY SUNDAY—"You will not have to be in Hell for five minutes until you will believe there is one."

SAM JONES—"The legitimate end of a sinful life is Hell."

You may say you still don't think so. It doesn't matter what you think or what I think; it's what God says that counts! Someone said, "The scholars have rejected the idea of Hell." When a scholar disagrees with God, that doesn't make God a liar and him right. In Romans 3:4 we read, ". . .Let God be true, but every man a liar."

Someone else said, "I believe hell is here on earth. If you are lost, this is all the heaven you will ever know. If you are saved, this is all of hell you will ever see." I will agree that there is plenty of hell on earth, but this has nothing to do with the Hell into which those who reject Christ will be cast. Those who have carelessly reasoned the matter out in their minds say, "God is too good to condemn man into a fire of Hell." Hebrews 12:29 says, "For our God is a consuming fire."

Let me point out incidents where God did and will use fire.

Genesis 19 tells how God rained down fire and brimstone on Sodom and Gomorrah.

In Leviticus 10:2, the two wicked sons of Aaron the priest put strange fire on the altar and the Bible says, "And there went out fire from the Lord, and devoured them, and they died before the Lord." We read in Numbers 11:1, "And when the people complained, it displeased the Lord: and the Lord heard it; and his anger was kindled; and the fire of the Lord burnt among them, and consumed them that were in the uttermost parts of the camp."

In Numbers God opened the earth and swallowed Korah and others. Then we read about those who remained alive, in Numbers 16:25, "And there came out a fire from the Lord, and consumed the two hundred and fifty men that offered incense." We read in II Kings 1:10 about the fire sent down from God in answer to Elijah's prayer and devoured fifty men, on two different occasions, who were trying to capture him for King Ahaziah.

Then in the New Testament, in II Thessalonians 1:7,8 we read, ". . .when the Lord Jesus shall be revealed from heaven with his mighty angels, In flaming fire taking vengeance on them that know not God, and that obey not the gospel of our Lord Jesus Christ." Second Peter 3:10 states, "The heavens shall pass away with a great noise, and the elements shall melt with fervent heat, the earth also and the works that are therein shall be burned up." Finally, in Revelation 20:15, "And whosoever was not found written in the book of life was cast into the lake of fire."

Now God has not changed and He has shown, in the Old Testament history and in the New Testament prophecy, that fire is His medium of judgment. I preach on Hell, because it's a moral necessity. Dr. John R. Rice's booklet, *Hell—What the Bible Says About It*, tells us on page 25,

> If God didn't send anybody to Hell, when we get to Heaven we would have to preach revivals to get sinners saved. You couldn't leave the door unlocked on your mansion, because all the thieves, crooks, bums, burglars and such would be there. You would witness funeral processions, because where there is sin there is death. You would find policemen to curtail crime, vice and drunkeness. You would see jails, war being waged by Hitler and insane asylums for the crazy.

Dr. Rice says, "God in Heaven, is that possible? No, thank God, it is not."

If the incidents of real life and newspaper accounts of tragedy by fire make us cringe when we read them, what will the misery and torments of Hell really be like? Our human mind is not capable of understanding either the blessings of Heaven or the horrors of Hell. Paul said, "Eye hath not seen, nor ear heard, neither have entered into the heart of man, the things which God hath prepared for them that love him" (I Cor. 2:9). I believe it is also true of Hell that it has not entered into a man's mind the things that God has prepared for them that reject Him.

According to the Scripture, both body and soul will be there. "And fear not them which kill the body, but are not able to kill the soul; but rather fear him which is able to destroy both soul and body in hell" (Matt. 10:29). The Scripture teaches that the wicked dead shall be raised to be judged and condemned to Hell.

It will be a place of wailing. Webster defines "wailing" as, "A cry or sound arising from grief or pain." I heard a man, in his last hours before death, crying with a hair-raising, mournful wail, in the hospital in Elkton, Maryland, some time ago and immediately I thought of this Bible term for the cry of Hell.

"There shall be wailing and gnashing of teeth" (Matt. 13:42). A dentist often tells a patient to grit his teeth before he injects a needle. Men will constantly grit their teeth because of pain.

When I was a boy there were several times when I had an aching tooth. I used to bite myself on the hand or finger to distract my attention from the pain of the tooth. In Hell, men will grit their teeth and gnaw on their flesh to try to ease suffering and pain. How awful! And yet, men blindly race on toward the pit.

Hell is a place of weeping. "There shall be weeping and gnashing of teeth" (Matt. 8:12). I don't believe that tears will flow, but dry, uncontrollable sobs will be heard ringing from every spot in Hell. Tears would mean water and certainly there is no water in Hell.

Hell is a place of torment. The rich man cried out, "I am tormented in this flame" (Luke 16:24). There will be the torment of bodily pain, blinding darkness and memories of the past.

Hell is a place of pitch darkness. Jesus said, "And cast ye the unprofitable servant into outer darkness." The man who stands in the barroom or pool hall and loudly boasts that he wants to go to Hell because his friends will be there needs to be reminded that if he bumped head on into his best friend, he would never know who it was. The darkness will cause fright and uncertainty and there will be stumbling, falling and a lost sense of balance. Jesus is the Light of the world and without Him there will be only darkness.

Hell is a place of unquenchable fire. In Mark 9:43-46 we find these words: ". . .into the fire that never shall be quenched." The hydrogen reaction of the sun continually erupting and never cooling is an example of a fire built by the Lord.

Hell is a place of memory. Abraham said to the rich man of our text, "Son, remember that thou in thy lifetime receivedst thy good things, and likewise Lazarus evil things. . . ." The lost man in Hell will remember the sermons he heard, the invitations he stood through, the tracts he read that were handed to him, the plea of loved ones to repent, and the opportunities God allowed for him to be saved. These memories will haunt him forever.

Hell is a place of thirst. The rich man cried, "Send Lazarus, that he may dip the tip of his finger in water, and cool my tongue. . . ." Not only will a man thirst for water, but every drinking man will crave liquor. The users of tobacco will cry out for just one cigarette. The lustful will have an uncontrollable desire that cannot be satisfied. For all eternity, men will reap what they have sown.

Hell is a place of passion for souls. The desire of the rich man was for someone to talk to his brothers, to warn them not to come to that horrible place. A mother in Hell does not want her boy to be there with her. She has the same cry, "Somebody tell my boy not to come here!" If the ones who love you the most are in Hell, they are pleading that you might be saved and miss the torment. .

Hell is a place of unanswered prayer. The rich man made his plea, but his prayer was never answered. Men may not pray now, but they will in Hell. Continually the cry of sinners in Hell will ring out, but, as in the days of Noah, God has shut the door and judgment has fallen.

The hypocrites will be there. Men excuse themselves from God's house because of the hypocrites that are there. Yet, they buy groceries for their families, gas for their car, work on the same jobs, and belong to the same clubs that the hypocrites do, but they are not about to go to church with them. This should be ever the more reason to be saved. . .to escape spending eternity with them!

Finally, Hell is forever. Men are not thinking about the length of eternity. How long is it? This is a crude example, but if you should be able to sum the number of grains of wheat that have ever been grown from the beginning of time, and multiply that enormous figure times all the leaves that have ever grown on all the trees since Adam's time, then multiply that figure times all the grains of sand on all the beaches of the world, then multiply that figure times all the people that have populated the earth since Adam's time, then multiply that figure times the stars in the sky, then multiply that times the number of inches to the sun, then multiply that times all the drops of rain that have ever fallen, times all the snowflakes that have floated to earth and then, multiply that times any number you can imagine times anything and everything that crosses your mind, when you are all finished, the number of years will not equal the end of eternity, but merely the beginning! The tragedy of it all is that some of you will spend all of that time in Hell!

HELL! THE PRISON HOUSE OF DESPAIR

Hell! The prison house of despair.
Here are some things that won't be there:
No flowers will bloom on the banks of Hell,
No beauties of nature we love so well;
No comforts of home, music and song,
No friendship of joy will be found in that throng;
No children to brighten the long, weary night;
No love nor peace, nor one ray of light;
No blood-washed soul with face beaming bright,

No loving smile in that region of night;
  No mercy, no pity, pardon nor grace,
No water; O God, what a terrible place!
  The pangs of the lost no human can tell,
Not one moment's ease—there is no rest in Hell!
  Hell! The prison house of despair,
Here are some things that will be there;
  Fire and brimstone are there, we know,
For God in His Word hath told us so;
  Memory, remorse, suffering and pain,
Weeping and wailing, but all in vain;
  Blasphemers, swearers, haters of God,
Christ-rejectors, while here on earth trod;
  Murderers, gamblers, drunkards and liars,
Will have their part in the lake of fire;
  The filthy, the vile, the cruel and mean,
What a horrible mob in Hell will be seen!
  Yes, more than humans on earth can tell,
Are torments and woes of Eternal Hell!

III. How to Escape Hell?

In Matthew 23:33, Jesus is talking to the scribes and Pharisees. He said, "How can ye escape the damnation of hell?" This question can only be answered one way—by accepting Jesus Christ as your personal Saviour and Lord.

Let us remember that God never intended for any of us to end up in Hell, according to Matthew 25:41. ". . .Depart from me, ye cursed, into everlasting fire, prepared for the devil and his angels." Hell was prepared for the Devil and his angels. Neither let us forget that the Lord is ". . .Not willing that any should perish, but that all should come to repentance" (II Pet. 3:9). John 3:16 also carries this same wonderful thought.

Jesus said that, if necessary, a man should pluck out his eye if it offended and was causing him to be lost. He added that it would be better for a man to cut off his hand or foot and go to Heaven than have them in this life and go to Hell, because of them. The greatest problem is not offending eyes, hands or feet, but neglect, procrastination and rejection. More people will be in Hell over these than the sins of murder, adultery and stealing.

In Hebrews 2:3, we are warned, "How shall we escape, if we

neglect so great salvation," and again in Proverbs 29:1, "He, that being often reproved hardeneth his neck, shall suddenly be destroyed, and that without remedy." God help you not to neglect or delay but respond to the knock of the Saviour on your heart and open the door by inviting Him in.

The way of escape is by simple, childlike faith, turning to Christ in repentance. Commit your past, present and future into His hands and, by faith, claim His promise of forgiveness and cleansing. Confess to Him that you are a sinner, call upon Him for forgiveness through the blood, claim the promise of salvation by faith, confess Him before men, and I'll meet you in Heaven.

This is the rich man's testimony, "And in hell he lift up his eyes, being in torments." This can be yours. . .'And in Heaven he lift up his eyes, being in glory.'

"Is There Any Word From the Lord?"

"When Jeremiah was entered into the dungeon, and into the cabins, and Jeremiah had remained there many days; Then Zedekiah the king sent, and took him out: and the king asked him secretly in his house, and said, Is there any word from the Lord?"—Jer. 37:16,17.

There certainly is a word from the Lord! Jeremiah didn't realize it, but he was speaking for all ages when he said, "THERE IS. . ." (Jer. 37:17b). In the Old Testament alone, more than 3,800 places state, "The word of the Lord came unto me" or some phrase parallel to it. There is a word from the Lord. In fact, there are 773,692 words from the Lord recorded in 31,173 verses, 1,189 chapters, 66 books and divided into two major divisions—the Old and New Testaments.

The Apostle Paul declared with great authority that, "All scripture is given by inspiration of God. . ." (II Tim. 3:16). There is great power in the message of the Lord. Paul declared, "For I am not ashamed of the gospel of Christ: for it is the power of God unto salvation to every one that believeth" (Rom. 1:16). Again he states, "For the preaching of the cross is to them that perish foolishness; but unto us which are saved it is the power of God" (I Cor. 1:18).

Ezekiel was commanded to preach the Word of the Lord to a valley full of dry bones (Ezek., chap. 37). No preacher ever had it any harder with a congregation than did Ezekiel. A lot of crowds are dead and unconcerned, but none could beat this! Every preacher who has thought of resigning because of a hard field needs to read that chapter in Ezekiel. There was no unity; the bones were scattered. There was no usefulness, for the lifeless pile of dusty bones was not going to accomplish anything. There wasn't any unction either. The Spirit had long since departed.

One can't help but notice the similarity between this pitiful picture and a lot of dead, dry, lifeless, formal churches going through the motions of worship. The crowd in the pews have little idea of what is going on, and they are glad when the service is over so they can get home to cut grass or wash the car. Usually the clergy is glad to get the chore over with so he can get an early start to the golf course or down to the boat.

But that can all be fixed by a good, clear word from the Lord. Ezekiel preached as he was commanded, and the bones began to unify. He preached again, this time to the wind just like God told him, and breath entered into the bodies and they came alive.

What we need more than anything else is for preachers and teachers to let people know what God has said, because *THERE IS* a word from the Lord. Jeremiah had the Word of the Lord burning in his heart. He knew there was a Word from the Lord, but on one occasion he got upset and quit. He vowed he would never preach again, or even mention the Lord's name. But God's message began to burn in his soul and he said, "But his word was in mine heart as a burning fire shut up in my bones, and I was weary with forbearing, and I could not stay" (Jer. 20:9).

I. It Will Save the Down-and-Out

No drunkard or harlot was ever too hard for God to save. Testimony is given around the world by those who lived vile, wicked, ungodly lives of how a message from God went to work in their heart and brought conviction and concern.

The Samaritan woman at the well was no Sunday school girl. She had changed husbands for the fifth time, and finally just didn't bother to marry the sixth. The message from Jesus about the water of life that would wash away all her sins was like a lightning bolt. She quickly pleaded, "Give me this water. . ."

(John 4:15). What she was saying was, "I'm tired of all this sin." If anyone was ever a down-and-outer, this woman was; but a Word from the Lord fixed it all up.

Blind Bartimaeus was a down-and-outer. He begged and pleaded for physical health. He was unhappy, bitter and pitiful. But a Word from the Lord sure changed things for him!

I remember when I tried to talk to a man who was an alcoholic. He was sitting in an old, dirty, black Ford along with four or five more drunks. He wouldn't work steady. His family suffered, but he just didn't seem to care. He was a typical down-and-outer. When he saw me coming, he slowly pulled away, with me yelling for him to stop, pretending not to see me. Later I caught up with him and we talked. I gave him a message from the Lord.

He was saved and soon was baptized and joined our church. Soon he got a good job, bought a car and home. He was elected superintendent of our Sunday school, then bus director and finally treasurer. He is one of the best-loved and respected men in the church today.

The Word of the Lord will save the down-and-outer.

II. It Will Save the Up-and-Out

John Wanamaker, J. C. Penney, Andrew Kraft, Cyrus McCormick and J. Pierpont Morgan, all millionaires, were said to have been born-again Christians. Nicodemus, a rich, religious ruler, came to Jesus to talk about being saved. He was an up-and-outer in the strictest sense. Jesus explained: "As Moses lifted up the serpent in the wilderness, even so must the Son of man be lifted up" (John 3:14). The message did its work and Nicodemus was saved.

Lydia, a seller of purple, listened to the preaching of Paul and Silas and became the first convert of Europe. This up-and-outer got in.

Jairus listened carefully to the message of Jesus, after his daughter was raised, and another up-and-outer became a believer.

The nobleman came seeking help for his dying son and found help for himself and his whole house.

Recently, during a revival meeting in a Southern state, I noticed a very quiet, dignified man sitting in the choir. He was there every night. He seemed to be the busiest man in the church. I asked the pastor who he was. "Oh, he's a banker," the pastor replied.

Praise the Lord for the salvation of up-and-outers!

III. It Will Stabilize the In-and-Out

Every pastor knows too well the problems of the loose, careless, lukewarm in-and-out type of church members. They are not regular in prayer, Bible study or attendance. They go in spurts and seasons. They need something and it is not easy to tell whether it is conversion or rededication. The remedy for this problem is the same plain preaching! Paul advised Timothy, "Preach the word; be instant in season, out of season. . ." (II Tim. 4:2).

Look what it did for *Denying Peter.* He meant well, but he cursed and swore, vowed that he never saw Jesus in his life. After some contact with the words of a departing Saviour, he went to the Upper Room and obeyed orders. Pentecost shows the difference as 3,000 came to Christ through a simple message from the Word.

Look again at *Doubting Thomas.* He was an in-and-outer. At a very significant time, he was out. He would not believe anything, but a few words from the Lord and he cried out, "My Lord and my God" (John 20:28).

Look at *Deceitful Ananias and Sapphira.* Barnabas had the real thing, but these folks were in-and-outers. They were only doing their deed because he had set the example. Then they backed out on their commitment to the Lord. The Word from the Lord did not help them, but it certainly did stabilize the rest of the early church. We read that, "And great fear came upon all the church, and upon as many as heard these things" (Acts 5:11).

Recently a local man went to the store to get a $69.00 check cashed. The clerk gave him the money, but later, in counting, he discovered he had $96.00. Somehow, the clerk had read the figures upside down. The man had been saved several years and, even though he had not been regular in church attendance, he maintained the standard instilled into his life during his walk with the Lord.

He discussed it with his wife and decided to return the money. The next day he died suddenly. Don't you know that, at the Judgment Seat, he will sure be glad he returned what was not his! The Word of God had stabilized him in time of testing.

IV. It Will Stir the Out-and-Out

Jeremiah was a good man of God. One day, while he was meditating on the Word from the Lord, he cried out, "But his word was in mine heart as a burning fire shut up in my bones . . ." (Jer. 20:9). The Words of the Lord are spirit and life. They will stir and arouse us out of lethargy and complacency and will feed and bless the faithful.

Contact with the message of the Lord will create a stronger burden in the heart of the saint. It will also clean up the sinful tendencies and patterns. Then it will comfort the troubled and bereaved. Paul told the Christians at Thessalonica, "Wherefore, comfort one another with these words" (I Thess. 4:18).

The story was told of a happy family of a mom, dad and two beautiful little girls. They wanted a little baby brother for the girls, and soon the desire was met. After the baby was born, the doctor took the parents aside and gave them the saddest word they had ever heard: the little fellow was crippled and deformed. It was a hard blow, but they were soon busy planning and caring for their family. After about three years, the boy learned to walk in a faltering way.

It was time for Daddy to come home. Mother suggested the girls meet him at the gate. They decided to pick a love bouquet for him. The little fellow saw them and went into the yard, found a dandelion and crushed it in his hand. Soon he found a broken stick and placed it into his bouquet. He fumbled, with a dirty string, to tie them together. "There's Daddy!" squealed one of the girls, and down the sidewalk and into his arms they went. He hugged them to himself with a daddy's joy. Then he saw the little fellow hobbling toward him with his love bouquet. It wasn't much, but it was the best he could do. With big tears streaming down his cheeks Dad ran to the boy and picked him up in his arms. This was the best gift of all!

Friend, we may not have much to offer, but, if we give our best, God will be pleased and accept it with great reward.

There is a Word from the Lord! Let us hear it, heed it and hurry!

Spiritual Pardon

"For I will be merciful to their unrighteousness; and their sins and their iniquities will I remember no more."—Heb. 8:12.

A man on death row, sweating it out, hoping, praying and waiting for a word of pardon from the governor's office, would be a fool to turn it down if it came.

Some years ago, in a Pennsylvania state penitentiary, this very thing happened. The public was shocked. The warden of the prison walked down death row. He came to the cell where a young man was waiting the coming hour of death. Excitement and tenseness filled the whole cell block as the warden broke the joyful news, "The governor has sent the pardon!"

"I don't want it! Let me alone. I want to die!" came the startling words from the man inside the cell. The young man refused all pleas and insisted on his right to die.

The law books were examined and a special legislature session was called to determine what action should be taken. The lawmakers concluded that a pardon must be accepted in order for it to be valid. The young prisoner, refusing to receive the pardon, paid the supreme penalty and went out to meet God.

Many have said, "He was crazy!" or "What a fool!" Perhaps they were right, but there are thousands of people who continually refuse God's offer of pardon from eternal second death.

Let us consider the following things:

I. God's Penalty

There is a vast difference between the state code and the law of

God. The state law says that a man is innocent until he is proven guilty. God's law tells us that ALL are guilty. We read, ". . .he that believeth not is condemned already. . ." (John 3:18). Romans 5:12 tells us, "Wherefore, as by one man sin entered into the world, and death by sin; and so death passed upon all men, for that all have sinned." "ALL" takes in the good and the bad. Paul says, "As it is written, There is none righteous, no, not one" (Rom. 3:10).

The Book of God's law has set the standard and we read, "For all have sinned, and come short of the glory of God" (Rom. 3:23). The same Book that records the law also records the penalty. The man who breaks God's commandment must pay the penalty. The penalty for a broken law is eternal death. In Revelation 20:14 the penalty is called "the second death" or "lake of fire." Romans 6:23 declares again, "For the wages of sin is death. . . ."

No mention is made of degrees of sin. The man who breaks the least is guilty of all. The man who breaks one commandment has broken all ten. "For whosoever shall keep the whole law, and yet offend in one point, he is guilty of all" (James 2:10). The liar is as bad as the murderer. The woman who takes God's name in vain is just as wicked as the harlot. The person who doesn't love his neighbor doesn't love God.

According to the Bible, everyone is guilty and the penalty is hanging over every head. Millions are sitting on death row. Some have quit drinking, cursing, lying, stealing and quit all the rest. Others have even joined churches and have been baptized. But all these are still condemned by the penalty. Will the pardon come? Will it be accepted?

II. God's Payment

Barabbas was a murderer. He was waiting on death row. The execution was to come soon. The jailer came and announced, "Barabbas, you are free!" Barabbas shouted for joy and couldn't believe his ears. What happened? Who arranged this? All the answers were wrapped up in a short statement, "Jesus is going to die instead of you."

Yes, Jesus took Barabbas' place and died for him. He was the payment. Romans 5:8 tells us, "But God commendeth his love toward us, in that, while we were yet sinners, Christ died for us." We also read, "And he is the propitiation for our sins: and not for our's only, but also for the sins of the whole world" (I John 2:2).

In the Old Testament, the sins of the people were placed on lambs and the lambs were slain. Blood was shed to make an atonement for sins. God promised them that if they just believed in His Word they were forgiven and cleansed for one year. In the New Testament, Jesus was the Lamb. His payment was made for all and He substituted as the Lamb. God has said that His sacrifice was our payment. By faith we believe it and relax.

III. God's Plea

One might think that folks would run over the top of one another to accept the payment for sin and pardon for guilt. To the contrary, men are unconcerned. Because of the Devil's influence, men have ignored God and have forgotten that they are on death row. The Bible says, "But if our gospel be hid, it is hid to them that are lost: In whom the god of this world hath blinded the minds of them which believe not, lest the light of the glorious gospel of Christ, who is the image of God, should shine unto them" (II Cor. 4:3,4).

But God is concerned. God loves men and is not willing that any should perish. Through the efforts of the Holy Spirit, the Lord is speaking, reminding and warning men of their need. God's plea is, "Come now, and let us reason together, saith the Lord: though your sins be as scarlet, they shall be as white as snow; though they be red like crimson, they shall be as wool" (Isa. 1:18). He pleads, "Come; for all things are now ready" (Luke 14:17). Again comes the call, "Come unto me, all ye that labour and are heavy laden, and I will give you rest" (Matt. 11:28). He again urges, "Take my yoke upon you. . ." (Luke 14:18). A note of warning is sounded, with the plea, "Seek ye the Lord while he may be found, call ye upon him while he is near" (Isa. 55:6).

IV. God's Promise

Man is condemned. God has provided a payment. Now, the Lord is pleading with the hearts of men to believe and receive His gift of salvation. The contract has been drawn up. God has made His list of promises. We find recorded, "And this is the promise that he hath promised us, even eternal life" (I John 2:25). Numbers 23:19 tells us, "God is not a man, that he should lie . . . ." The Word of God is true and safe. Surely, man can believe what God has said.

God has promised to give the gift of eternal pardon and salvation to all who would receive it. God has promised that, "For whosoever shall call upon the name of the Lord shall be saved" (Rom. 10:13). Again He has said, ". . .him that cometh to me I will in no wise cast out" (John 6:37). The man who has been saved has believed the promise of God, and the man who is still lost has not, as yet, believed God.

V. God's Pardon

Now, what is contained in this pardon? Are there any strings attached? May I assure you, dear reader, there is no kidding here. This is not the time of foolishness. It is a serious business for a man to be condemned.

First, notice that pardon is not penance. Deciding to turn over a new leaf, or saying, "I'll not do it anymore," will not get the prisoner out of jail. Many are laying aside their evil deeds and striving to live better lives. Some already have sown their wild oats and now they feel that good, moral living will get them through the gate of Heaven.

Penance is trying to reform, or trying to make up for sin, by doing good. The rich man pays the bills of the church to get God to overlook how he made his money. The sincere society woman serves on all the committees and labors long to try to repay her evil acts in former days. But, this is the work of the flesh. "Therefore by the deeds of the law there shall no flesh be justified in his sight. . ." (Rom. 3:19). "Not by works of righteousness which we have done, but according to his mercy he saved us. . ." (Titus 3:5).

Secondly, please notice that pardon is not parole. The pardoned man is free, while the paroled man is under conditions. If the man who is on parole gets into any trouble at all, he must go back and serve the original sentence. To be pardoned suggests that all guilt is stricken from the record. A cloak of innocence is given to the pardoned man.

Many today believe that the child of God is on a conditional parole. They accept that we have been made free by our Substitute, but they declare that if we do not hold out, we will be taken back to judgment and end up paying the penalty in Hell.

My friend, God's pardon is eternal and the man who realizes it lives for God, through thankfulness. The convict is not just released; he is changed into a Christian.

Thirdly, notice that pardon is not payment. When a man has served out his sentence and released, there is no pardon involved. If he pays his fine and goes free, there is no need for mercy or pardon. Man does not have enough money to pay the fine. It would take eternity to serve out the sentence! The only hope is a full pardon. The Bible says, "If the Son therefore shall make you free, ye shall be free indeed" (John 8:36).

Pardon is available for you, dear sinner, just for the asking. God would be happy to forgive you and save you now. Just bow your head, commit yourself to Him and ask for spiritual pardon.

Heaven

"Behold, the heaven and heaven of heavens cannot contain thee. . . ."—I Kings 8:27.

". . .And hear thou in heaven thy dwelling place. . . ."—I Kings 8:30.

There are three different heavens discussed in the Bible. First, there is the atmosphere just above the earth. Second, there is the stellar heaven containing the stars amd planets. Finally, we have what the Bible calls "the third heaven." The third Heaven is where God's throne is located. It is the place called Paradise, where the saints of God are waiting for the resurrection of their bodies.

There are windows in Heaven and also a door. The windows are always spoken of as being open to pour out things from God. Sometimes blessings are poured out (see Mal. 3:10; II Kings 7:2), sometimes curses (see Isa. 24:18), and sometimes the same thing that is a blessing to some and a curse to others (see Gen. 8:2).

Concerning the door in Heaven, John tells of his experience in Revelation. "After this I looked, and, behold, a door was opened in heaven: and the first voice which I heard was as it were of a trumpet talking with me; which said, Come up hither, and I will shew thee things which must be hereafter" (Rev. 4:1).

The first thing he saw was a throne. This is God's throne. He was sitting on His throne. He looked like a jasper, sardine or an emerald. It is hard for the finite mind to grasp infinite things. We cannot imagine the beauty and radiance of God.

Recently we visited the Smithsonian Institute in Washington,

D.C. and saw the famous Hope Diamond. A thick, shatterproof glass wall and an armed guard protected it. The many people that waited in line to see it expressed awe, and a feeling of rapture seemed to come over all who viewed it. A spirit of excitement was presently set off by the thought of the tremendous value. But, this is nothing, this is dirt compared to God.

The psalmist cried out, "The Lord is in his holy temple, the Lord's throne is in heaven. . ." (Ps. 11:4). Behind the throne was a sparkling rainbow. The twenty-four elders, clothed with glistening, white garments and pure gold crowns on their heads, were seated upon the twenty-four seats. Thunder and lightnings were proceeding out from the throne and voices could be heard. There were seven lamps of fire burning before the throne.

The Tree of Life was there. This same tree was in the Garden of Eden for Adam and Eve. After the fall of man, an angel was posted at the gate with a revolving sword, to keep them away from this tree lest they should eat of it and live forever in their fallen state. On this tree grew twelve different kinds of fruit each month. The leaves were for the healing of the nations.

The beautiful River of Life was flowing out from under the throne and pure water of life was freely accessible. The streets were made of pure, transparent gold, suggesting the elimination of all impurities which cloud things on the earth.

As John continued to look, he saw twelve gates of pearl; three on the north, three on the south, three on the east and three on the west.Twelve angels stood at these twelve gates.

There will be no tears, no death, no sorrow, no crying, no pain, no night, no more curse, no hunger, no thirst or hundreds of other things that have plagued us here. The great host of angels, or messengers, will be busy serving God and carrying out every desire. When Jesus was born in Bethlehem, God sent a multitude of angels to earth to praise and cry out, "Glory to the Lord!" Surely, it must have been a great blessing for John to see all of this.

Stephen had been privileged to look on this scene, too. As he was dying, after being stoned, he spoke of seeing Jesus standing on the right hand of God. Before he could tell much of what he saw, God called him Home.

Paul the apostle got a glimpse of this on the Damascus Road. The vision was so bright, in contrast to his sin, that it blinded him. He later spoke to Herod Agrippa, saying, "Whereupon, O King Agrippa, I was not disobedient unto the heavenly vision" (Acts 26:19). Later, Paul tells of an experience of ascending up to the third Heaven. "I knew a man in Christ above fourteen years ago. . .such an one caught up to the third heaven. . . . How that he was caught up into paradise, and heard unspeakable words, which it is not lawful for a man to utter" (II Cor. 12:2,4).

Enoch and Elijah were taken up into Heaven. They saw the scene, but never returned to explain about it. Moses got a little glimpse of God, and his face shone with brilliance.

It is certainly going to be an amazing thing to go there and see for ourselves. We are told, "For we know that if our earthly house of this tabernacle were dissolved, we have a building of God, an house not made with hands, eternal in the heavens" (II Cor. 5:1).

God looks down from Heaven and sees. He also hears, as do others there. "The Lord looked down from heaven upon the children of men, to see if there were any that did understand, and seek God" (Ps. 14:2). We are reminded, "If my people, which are called by my name, shall humble themselves, and pray, and seek my face, and turn from their wicked ways; then will I hear from heaven, and will forgive their sin, and will heal their land" (II Chron. 7:14).

In Hebrews 12:1, we are cautioned, "Wherefore seeing we also are compassed about with so great a cloud of witnesses, let us lay aside every weight. . . ." The writer is saying that there are great multitudes of spectators in Heaven watching us in this life. They are called a "great cloud of witnesses."

There are several definite things that will be involved in going to Heaven. Notice these following things:

I. Review

The first thing on the schedule, after getting there, is the Judgment Seat. Paul explains, "For we must all appear before the judgment seat of Christ; that every one may receive the things done in his body, according to that he hath done, whether it be good or bad" (II Cor. 5:10). Following this will be the great Marriage Feast of the Lamb, revealed in Revelation 19:7. Only the saved will be involved in these. Here, every man's work will be tested by fire to see what sort it is. Sincere dedication will pay great dividends on this day.

II. Records

Heaven is a place of records. There will be record books at the Judgment Seat and at the Great White Throne Judgment. God has a great recording system to preserve every idle word, thought or deed. Scientists are working on a machine now that will use radio-active material to bring voices out of rocks and trees, that were recorded there hundreds of years ago by sound wave impressions. Be sure that God has things recorded.

We are told to rejoice because of this. "But rather rejoice, because your names are written in heaven" (Luke 10:20). In Hebrews, we read, "To the general assembly and church of the firstborn, which are written in heaven. . ." (Heb. 12:23). Pity the poor soul whose name is not written there!

John tells us, "And whosoever was not found written in the book of life was cast into the lake of fire" (Rev. 20:15).

III. Rewards

Heaven is a place of rewards. Jesus, speaking in the Sermon on the Mount, said, "Rejoice and be exceeding glad; for great is your reward in heaven. . ." (Matt. 5:12). He went on to say, "But lay up for yourselves treasures in heaven, where neither moth nor rust doth corrupt, and where thieves do not break through nor steal" (Matt. 6:20). This is our heavenly safe deposit box. There will be rewards for sincerity, suffering and service. To think along this line will excite the heart.

IV. Rejoicing

There will be much eternal joy in Heaven. The greatest joy that comes to Heaven is because of souls coming to Christ. "I say unto you, that likewise joy shall be in heaven over one sinner that repenteth, more than over ninety and nine just persons, which need no repentance" (Luke 15:7). Surely a great shout of joy can be heard from the redeemed saints when souls are saved. The Father, Son, Holy Spirit and angels must join with them to celebrate. "Therefore rejoice, ye heavens, and ye that dwell in them. . ." (Rev. 12:12).

V. Reunion

David remarked when his baby died, ". . .I shall go to him, but he shall not return to me" (II Sam. 12:23). Jesus promised, ". . .that where I am, there ye may be also" (John 14:3). It will be a homecoming time, and renewing old acquaintances will be exciting. Friends and loved ones already there will be out to meet us. We will meet those whom we have known from the Scriptures, such as Moses, Abraham and David. Then, it will be worth it all when we see Christ!

But, let every reader remember. . .the prepared place is for a prepared people.

A man may go to Heaven. . .

. . .without health
. . .without wealth
. . .without fame
. . .without name
. . .without learning
. . .without earnings
. . .without culture
. . .without beauty
. . .without friends
. . .without a thousand other things;

but, he cannot go to Heaven without Christ!

Why not make sure right now? Just bow your head and simply ask Jesus to come into your heart and save you. Write me and tell me about it.

Climbing Steps

"A man's heart deviseth his way: but the Lord directeth his steps."—Prov. 37:23.

"The steps of a good man are ordered by the Lord: and he delighteth in his way."—Ps. 37:23.

When our family moved to Pennsylvania, I was enrolled in the sixth grade at Kennett Square. My home room was on the third floor of the school building. Mrs. Fogg was waiting with folded arms at the bottom. To my utter embarrassment, she called out, "Tommy Wallace! You go back up those stairs and come down them right!" In my humiliation and desire to redeem myself, I hurried back up, three at a time. I heard from Mrs. Fogg again. In a frustrated tone, she demanded, "Tommy Wallace, you come down those steps right, go back up them right and come down them right again." I had had enough; she had, too. I could tell that she was getting serious. I carefully placed my foot on each step—all thirteen of them. Down, up, then down again I went, while the class giggled. Mrs. Fogg frowned and my face got redder and redder. I learned a valuable lesson that day.

God has a program and design for each life. His plan includes many steps that will bring us into conformity with His will. Steps of sickness, problems, testings and crises are found along the way. It is essential, then, that we use them all.

Let us examine some of the steps that lead to happiness in your personal life, heavenliness in your home life, and harmony in your church life.

I. Happiness in Your Personal Life

The psalmist stated, "Happy is that people. . .whose God is the Lord" (Ps. 144:15). Real happiness, of course, is always conditional. First, notice that *salvation* is necessary. Men, who are uncertain about eternity, will not be able to relax. The prospect of losing the soul is a nagging thought. The possibility of a lake of fire will drain the fun out of a thinking and reasonable mind. The presence of the Lord in our lives is necessary, too. The Holy Spirit comes into the body of the believer and dwells there.

Notice that *surrender* to God's will is important. A fierce battle is fought between the old nature and the new man. There can be no true happiness until the new man is in complete control. Paul spoke of this in Philippians: ". . .for I have learned, in whatsoever state I am, therewith to be content" (4:11). He explained in I Corinthians, "But I keep under my body, and bring it into subjection" (9:27).

Then *sacrifice* is involved. It seems strange that sacrifice, cost, price, demand, give, go and words like these lead to happiness. Jesus said that the way to live is to die; the way to have is to give, and the way to revival is travail. "For whosoever will save his life shall lose it: and whosoever will lose his life for my sake shall find it" (Matt. 16:25).

Finally, we see that *separation* is included. Happiness depends on who you run with and who you associate with. Those who associate with evil will want evil. Those who hang around the world will be worldly. We must walk with God to be godly. Those who would be spiritual, must be in regular contact and fellowship with the Spirit. "Come out," "Be not conformed," "Love not the world," "Have no fellowship," are just a few phrases we find in God's Word that show us God's desire for His children.

To be happy, obey His commands and desires. Do not miss any of these important steps!

II. Heavenliness in Your Home Life

Everyone wants a happy home. Love and companionship in the family circle is worth far more than gold, silver or world recognition. When you are tired, sick or discouraged, there is no place like home. It's not the carpet, furniture or fancy brick, but love that counts. What makes a G.I. in Viet Nam hunger to come home? Why do we always want to go back to Grandma's house at Thanksgiving and Christmas? That's home, and we are looking for happiness.

First, it is found in *family devotions*. When there is a daddy who will call the family together and read the Book of God, the home will be happy. There must be a mother who is not ashamed of the tear slipping down her face while she prays that God will use her boy and protect her girl. There will be children who will honor Mother and Father because of God's command that they should do so. This makes for a happy home.

Then, it is found in *fatherly discipline*. A child in rebellion and delinquency will rip the happiness out of a home and replace it with tears and broken hearts. Nothing cuts a heart like a wayward child.

The wise writer of Proverbs gives advice to head this off: "Withhold not correction from the child. . ." (22:13). "Train up a child in the way he should go. . ." (22:6). "The blueness of a wound cleanseth away evil. . ." (20:30). "Chasten thy son while there is hope. . ." (19:18).

Heavenliness in your home life is also found in *faithful dedication*. A home is worth dedication, and a dad who dedicates himself to fulfilling the office of high priest will not regret it. He is to lead in the church attendance, family worship and consistent living. The mother is to picture the bride in subjection to her Lord, maintaining purity, devotion and service in the home. The children are to obey, for this is well-pleasing to the Lord. The happy home is dependent upon these steps.

III. Harmony in Your Church

Harmony in a local assembly does not come by accident. The church at Jerusalem had it; the church at Corinth did not. The disciples met in unity and in one accord. It is not surprising to read about their experiences being described with such words as "gladness" and "praising God." They had peace toward God, purity toward their fellow-Christians and power toward the unbelievers. If a church is to have harmony, they must follow certain steps.

First, there must be *plain preaching.* The theme will need to be The Book, The Blood and The Blessed Hope. Men like Elijah, John the Baptist and Paul would not go over very well in our day, but they sure could do us good! "Preach the word; be instant in season, out of season. . ." (II Tim. 4:2). That is preaching when folk like it and when they don't like it!

I don't believe I'll ever forget my mother's old proverb, "It's not what you like that does you good." That old rag soaked in kerosene and smeared with lard was miserable around your neck all night, but it got rid of that sore throat. The kids hated castor oil, but it did the trick.

The medicine is not the only thing that has been sugar-coated. The preaching is dainty and pretty now. Preachers ought to get fighting mad when some little old lady comes up after the message and says, "That was a nice little talk, Preacher."

Secondly, there must be *praying people.* Someone said, "No praying, no power; little praying, little power; much praying, much power." It is the closet praying that counts. Jesus rose up a great while before daybreak and went out to pray alone. He knew He would not be bothered early.

> Few will come before God's throne,
>   Their heart's desires to Him make known.
> Few there are who seem to care,
>   Few there are who work at prayer.

How much do you pray? How long do you pray? How often do you pray? This is one of the steps.

Then, notice that *personal participation* is needed. They "all" with one accord met in the Upper Room. We are individual ambassadors, either a missionary or a mission field. In the Bible, words like "go," "daily," "from house to house," and "They ceased not to teach and preach Jesus Christ," refer to people, not churches.

A few years ago, when we were having between 400 and 500

each Sunday, an effort was made to get over 800. We organized together and asked our people to be responsible for bringing a certain number to Sunday school. A great host of people volunteered, and out among friends and neighbors we went. The enthusiasm was high. A revival spirit was in the air.

Then, late Saturday night it began to snow. It snowed all night and the reports came over the radio: we had five inches, then six, seven, and finally eight inches. We were heartsick. Our hopes were gone and the day ruined.

But when we got to Sunday school the people began to come— a great host of them! When the count of 864 came from the office, we rejoiced exceedingly! The people had worked and God had honored their work.

God's plan will always work if we follow His steps. It matters not if it be in the life, the home or the church; if it's done in God's way, He will bless it.

Is there a failure as you read these words? Have you been going at it in your own way? Why not come to God and tell Him right now that you will do the right thing? We have such a few days left to serve the Saviour. Let's do it right and with all our heart.

"Count It All Joy"

One of the songwriters has written, "If you want joy, real joy, wonderful joy. . .let Jesus come into your heart."

James makes it sound so easy. "My brethren, count it all joy when ye fall into divers temptations" (James 1:2). The "all" here means everything that could possibly come our way. Paul urged the Thessalonians, "Rejoice evermore" (I Thess. 5:16). He told the Philippians, "Rejoice in the Lord alway: and again I say, Rejoice" (Phil. 4:4).

Jesus said of His disciples, ". . .And these things I speak in the world, that they might have my joy fulfilled in themselves" (John 17:13). John said, "And these things write we unto you, that your joy may be full" (I John 1:4).

Let us notice five areas of joy.

I. Joy in the Scriptures

There was great singing for joy when Pharaoh and his army were drowned in the Red Sea. Hannah said, "My heart rejoiceth in the Lord. . ." when little Samuel was born (I Sam. 2:1). Naomi was thrilled and rejoiced when Boaz took Ruth as his wife. Israel shouted for joy when Saul was crowned king. The streets were filled with women singing and shouting for joy when David killed the giant and the soldiers came home.

There was a time of great joy and celebrating when the captured Ark of the Covenant was brought home to God's people. All Israel joined in the rejoicing at the dedication of the Temple.

Nehemiah led the people in a time of great joy when the city walls were finished. Esther, Mordecai and all the Jews were filled with joy when Haman hanged on his evil gallows. The birth of Christ was an occasion of joy to the angels, the shepherds, Mary and the others.

When the prodigal son came home, a joyful celebration was held. The followers of Jesus cried, "Hosanna" or "Joy to the Highest," when He rode into Jerusalem. There was great joy at Pentecost. The impotent man leaped with joy after the healing of his body. Paul and Silas rejoiced and sang praises at midnight in the Philippian jail.

On and on the story goes. The Scriptures are filled with incidents that brought joy to multitudes.

II. Joy in Salvation

When Philip brought revival to the city of Samaria, many turned to Christ and we read, "And there was great joy in that city" (Acts 8:8). In the story of the prodigal son, we clearly see the joy of salvation. Notice, first, the father's joy. ". . .his father saw him, and had compassion, and ran, and fell on his neck, and kissed him" (Luke 15:20). This pictures God, ". . .not willing that any should perish, but that all should come to repentance" (II Pet. 3:9). The Lord rejoices when sinners come home.

Notice, too, that the neighbors and friends rejoiced. He called them to come and rejoice with him. In our church where people are saved all the time we have become far too complacent. There should be weeping and rejoicing for a long time after a service when someone has started for Heaven.

Thirdly, see the angels of Heaven rejoicing. They really get excited in Heaven over one repentant sinner. ". . .joy shall be in heaven over one sinner that repenteth, more than over ninety and nine just persons, which need no repentance" (Luke 15:7).

Then, notice the sinner's joy. What a relief and blessing to get the load of sin off your back! This poor, sinful boy came back fully expecting to be a bond servant, but ended up as a son again.

Oh, happy day that fixed my choice,
On Thee, my Saviour and my God.
Well may this glowing heart rejoice,
And tell its raptures all abroad.

III. Joy in Service

The Queen of Sheba came to visit Solomon. She had heard of all the glory of his kingdom. When she saw for herself, she said "Happy are thy men, happy are these thy servants were happy. There is a joy in service. The servants of the Lord Jesus are happy, too! Isaiah 65:14 speaks of, ". . .my servants shall sing for joy of heart. . . ."

Solomon said, "There is nothing better for a man, than that he should eat and drink, and that he should make his soul enjoy good in his labour" (Eccles. 2:24). David said, "I delight to do thy will, O my God. . ." (Ps. 40:8). Someone has said, "Happy is the man whose occupation becomes his hobby."

Several years ago in our church some forty or fifty of our men entered into a program of volunteer service to maintain buildings and buses. They worked with joy and blessing day after day and night after night. Oftentimes these men said they would not do the same work for money, but they would do it for the Lord.

IV. Joy in Sorrow

"Your sorrow shall be turned into joy" (John 16:20). Jesus spoke of a woman in travail and sorrow because her hour was come, "But as soon as she is delivered of the child, she remembereth no more the anguish, for joy that a man is born into the world" (John 16:21).

Paul continually emphasized this great truth. "As sorrowful, yet always rejoicing" (II Cor. 6:10); "I am filled with comfort, I am exceeding joyful in all our tribulation" (II Cor. 7:4). Jesus reminded His disciples, "In the world ye shall have tribulation: but be of good cheer; I have overcome the world" (John 16:33).

The psalmist said that "weeping may endure for a night, but joy cometh in the morning" (Ps. 30:5).

V. Joy in Soul Winning

Angels rejoice more over people being saved than anything else. Surely, we ought to agree with them in this matter. "They that sow in tears shall reap in joy" (Ps. 126:5). "He that goeth forth and weepeth, bearing precious seed, shall doubtless come again with rejoicing, bringing his sheaves with him" (vs. 6).

There was great joy when the lost son came home, when the lost coin was found and when the lost sheep returned.

The dear Lord wants us to have joy in our heart and life at all times. The result of dedicated obedience is a filling of the Spirit and the fruit of the Spirit—JOY.

What Makes a
Church Great?

"And with great power gave the apostles witness of the resurrection of the Lord Jesus: and great grace was upon them all."—
Acts 4:33.

This great church at Jerusalem is our God-given example of *"how to do it."* These folk got in touch with Heaven, received their orders and the power to carry them out and please God. In this day, when hundreds of churches are like dead batteries, giving out their sermonettes to Christianettes by preacherettes so they can get out and smoke their cigarettes, we need some prophets who will stand like the Rock of Gibraltar and build a mighty fortress for God.

Let me share with you seven things that made the early New Testament church one of the greatest the world has ever known.

I. They Had a Great Purpose

Their purpose was to obey the Saviour. Jesus had asked them to tarry in the Upper Room. He said, "But tarry ye in the city of Jerusalem, until ye be endued with power from on high" (Luke 24:49). Obedience is always a vital link to power and blessing from God. Someone has said, "It is not ours to reason why; it is but ours to do or die."

Then, their purpose was to obtain the promise. The promise, of course, was the blessed Holy Spirit. Jesus had promised in Acts 1:8, "But ye shall receive power, after that the Holy Ghost is come upon you. . . ." This promise is made to every person who desires to receive it from the Lord.

Their purpose was to offer the Gospel. They were to be witnesses. . ."both in Jerusalem, and in all Judaea, and in Samaria, and unto the uttermost part of the earth" (Acts 1:8). Peter stood before the great crowd in the streets of Jerusalem and offered the Gospel to the Jews from many nations. The sermon was simple and his purpose was plain. He wanted to help people get to Heaven.

II. They Had Great Preaching

Peter was an ordinary man and not really a great preacher, but his sermon was great preaching. Great preaching in the early church had a threefold characteristic: it *exalted* Christ, it *edified* the Christians and it *exposed* sin. These great characteristics are present in all great sermons.

Jesus promised that the Holy Spirit, when He was come, would reprove the world of sin or expose it and reveal righteousness to the world, which was exalting Christ and would explain the purpose of the cross and the judging of Satan. Three thousand people responded to the invitation and then five thousand, at a later sermon. No one can deny that this is great preaching!

III. They Had Great Power

The power at Pentecost was the same used at creation, to divide the Red Sea, to keep Daniel safe in the lions' den, and to rescue the three Hebrew children from the fiery furnace. This was also the same power that turned the water to wine, healed the nobleman's son, fed the five thousand, gave sight to the blind man and raised Lazarus from the dead.

This great power was manifest in the streets of Jerusalem that day and is available to every Christian who will seek God and pay the price. Notice this power depends on certain things. It is dependent upon a *clean life.* God will not fill a dirty vessel with His Holy Spirit power. We must be clean. It depends on *consistent walking.* Jesus is the same yesterday, today and forever. The fly-by-night, blow-hot-blow-cold, in-and-out kind of Christianity does not know the power of God.

Then, great power depends on *continual asking.* Jesus said, "If a son shall ask bread of any of you that is a father, will he give him a stone? or if he ask a fish, will he for a fish give him a serpent?. . .How much more shall your heavenly Father give the Holy Spirit to them that ask him?" (Luke 11:11,13). Surely God will not refuse those who know how to die and can tell others. "See that ye refuse not him that speaketh. . ." (Heb. 12:25), for then you shall be in danger of hearing the words of this text, ". . . I have refused him" (I Sam. 16:7).

The Recruiting of David

With Saul rejected and Eliab refused, we are delighted to see David recruited to do the job! God knew this boy's heart. David had a willing heart. When the Lord looked into his heart, He saw a boy. . ."after his own heart" (I Sam. 13:14). His motives were pure, his life was clean and he was ready to go where the Lord led.

David also had a *wise head.* He was wise enough to wait until the proper time to claim the throne. His experience of victory over the bear and the lion, as well as over Goliath, expresses a note of wisdom.

David had *working hands.* Notice that out of eight boys, he was the one working. This is an indication that he was more suited to be king. When the Lord recruits His workers, surely these areas of the heart, the head and the hands are of major importance. He is looking for a clean heart, a clear head and calloused hands.

The story is told of a rich farmer in Greece who was about to die. He told both of his sons that he had buried his treasures in the fields. Before he could tell which field, he passed away.

The boys began to dig and turn the soil. For weeks they worked, seeking treasures. At last and near exhaustion, they realized that planting time was upon them. Since they had literally plowed the fields with their digging, they agreed to plant and wait until after the harvest to dig again.

The fruit yield came forth, in great abundance, because of the deep turning of the soil. It was then that they awoke to the wisdom of their father. He had inspired them to work and labor in the fields and they had found a great treasure of wealth. ". . .Look on the fields; for they are white already to harvest . . ." (Matt. 9:38).

The story is told of a huge barge loaded with brick and rock that sank in a New York harbor. Over a long period of years, it had mired deep in the mud, sinking a little more each year from weight. The engineers, attempting to build a large bridge across the body of water, were hindered by this barge, because it was necessary to plant a foundation in that very spot. All their efforts and machinery could not do the job.

Finally, a young engineer came up with an idea and they gave it a try. Several big barges were chained together and floated into the area at low tide. Several chains were hooked to the sunken barge and then, they backed off to wait. As the tide began to rise, there was a creaking, groaning, and snapping of chains. Soon the barge broke loose and was lifted out of its place and floated away. The power of the Atlantic Ocean had been used to raise the barge.

Surely, there is an example here for us. When all efforts of human wisdom fail, God's mighty power can do the job!

IV. They Had Great Persecution

It is sad that those who do the work of God upon the earth are persecuted, but this is history. Christians have always been persecuted. Jesus said to His disciples, "In the world ye shall have tribulation. . ." (John 16:33). The Apostle Paul promised, "If we suffer, we shall also reign with him. . ." (II Tim. 2:12).

These early Christians went through deep waters, and eleven of the twelve apostles were killed in a violent way. When people really go all out to please God, there will be criticism and threatening, as there was in the early New Testament church.

The chief priests and scribes tried to stamp out this early religion. It even included imprisonment. Peter was thrown into jail, as were some of the others. Finally, Herod killed James and would have killed Peter, too, had not the Lord spared him. Stephen was stoned to death. All except John were martyred for their faith in Christ. John was exiled to Patmos, where he wrote the Book of Revelation.

V. They Had Great People

The people in this early Christian group were those willing to give up their very life's work. Peter left his nets and followed Jesus. James and John were willing to forsake their fishing business and become fishers of men. These folk were willing to give up their wealth. Barnabas sold his house and laid his money at the offering table to be used for the work of God. They were willing to give up their very life. Stephen was willing to lay down his life in the street and give up his soul unto the Lord.

What a blessing to look out over the congregation of people at our church and see those who have been willing to do these very same things to further the cause of Christ. It takes great people to make a great church. People are the church, not the building.

VI. They Had Great Praise

We read that, "They continued daily with one accord. . . Praising God, and having favour with all the people. . ." (Acts 2:46,47). As miracles took place, such as the healing of the blind man at the gate of the beautiful Temple, all of the people joined him in praising God. David must have caught the spirit of this when he wrote Psalm 107. Five times he cried out in this Psalm, "Oh that men would praise the Lord for his goodness, and for his wonderful works to the children of men!"

There ought to be great praise to God for the Gospel, and for His willingness to endure the death, burial and resurrection, in order to provide redemption for sinners. Then, there is a need for praise for His goodness. How good God is! "But God commendeth his love toward us, in that, while we were yet sinners, Christ died for us" (Rom. 5:8). There ought to be great praise for God's grace. It is by this grace that we are saved, and by His mercy has He saved us.

One shabby, little old lady with gray hair listened to the testimonies of people in the church about the goodness of God. She stood to her feet and said, "I don't have much of this world's goods. My health is not so good. I only have two teeth, one up and one down; but, praise God, they meet!" This certainly ought to be the attitude of all true Christians. There is always something to be thankful for.

VII. They Had Great Promises

These people had a promise of Heaven, and so do we. These people had a promise of the Holy Spirit, and so do we. They had a promise of genuine happiness, and so do we. "And this is the promise that he hath promised us, even eternal life" (I John 2:25). Thousands of promises in the Bible are for your benefit and mine.

Surely the need of this day is to analyze carefully these seven great things that this great early church had, apply them to our situation and benefit, that we, too, might have a great church for a great God.

Soul Winning

"Jesus saith unto them, My meat is to do the will of him that sent me and to finish his work. Say not ye, There are yet four months, and then cometh harvest? Behold, I say unto you, Lift up your eyes, and look on the fields; for they are white already to harvest."—John 4:34,35.

"After these things the Lord appointed other seventy also, and sent them two and two before his face into every city and place, whither he himself would come. Therefore said he unto them, the harvest truly is great, but the labourers are few: pray ye therefore the Lord of the harvest, that he would send forth labourers into his harvest."—Luke 10:1,2.

"They that sow in tears shall reap in joy. He that goeth forth and weepeth, bearing precious seed, shall doubtless come again with rejoicing, bringing his sheaves with him."—Ps. 126:5,6.

"The fruit of the righteous is a tree of life; and he that winneth souls is wise."—Prov. 11:30.

Sinners are everywhere. Like ripened fields of standing grain, they wait for someone to come in mercy and bring the harvest in.

> **Bring them in, Bring them in,**
> **Bring them in from the fields of sin.**
> **Bring them in, Bring them in.**
> **Bring the wandering ones to Jesus.**

Andrew brought his brother to Christ. Philip helped the eunuch get saved. Peter led Cornelius and his whole family to the Lord. Paul showed Lydia, the Philippian jailer, Timothy and many others what to do. Jesus personally dealt with the Samaritan woman, Nicodemus, Zacchaeus and a multitude of others.

The Bible clearly shows that people are everywhere and the Gospel is their only hope. The great need is for those who have the light to share it with those in darkness. ". . .And how shall they believe in him of whom they have not heard? And how shall they hear without a preacher [witness]?" (Rom. 10:14). Thousands of people would like to be saved if Christians would only take time to help them.

I remember visiting with one of our bus pastors on Saturday several months ago. Every one we saw that day was busy. Nobody wanted to talk to a preacher. One man told us he didn't have time to worry about Heaven; he had to fix his car so he could get to work on Monday. We made 17 visits and didn't get to first base.

I was ready to give up, but the bus pastor insisted on one more house. "This is a new family," he said. They had just moved in. We knocked on the door and a lady answered. It turned out that she was an old friend of the bus pastor. They talked of old times a moment. Then he asked her about her church interest and relationship to the Lord. She broke into tears and explained that she had been to church the last two Sundays, trying to get saved. In just a moment we led her to Christ. She had been out there all the time with a hungry heart. All we had to do was find her. I'm convinced that they are everywhere.

I. Some Are in the Hospital

I walked into a hospital ward, introduced myself and explained that I had come to pray for them. One lady mentioned that she lived near our church, so I invited her to visit us. "I'll not be there," she blurted out. "I'm a Quaker," she declared, "and we don't go to other churches." I tried to be friendly and explained that we would still like for her to come. She flatly told me again, "I'll not come."

The lady in the next bed was very nervous and was crying. She asked me to pray for her and tell her how she could be right with the Lord. She committed herself to Christ and seemed to relax. The next day I went back and the woman who said she would not be there remarked, "I'm glad you are back. I want you to 'change me over.' "

"Do *what* to you?" I asked.

"You know, change me over. Make a Baptist out of me."

I explained that it was a Christian she needed to be and not just a Baptist. She was sweetly converted. They are everywhere.

II. These Two Were Waiting in the Hall

A young couple was in tears. I explained that I was a preacher and asked if I might help. "Our baby is dying in there, Preacher. Please pray!"

"Can you pray?" I asked them.

"No, we are not saved," they answered.

"Don't you think that three of us could pray more effectively than just one?" I suggested. They agreed. I explained the gospel story and we prayed. They were soundly converted.

The baby died and went to Heaven, but two more children were born to them and they have both been saved. Now there is one in Heaven and four more going because of God's wisdom. I'm so glad I found them in the hall.

III. They Wanted to Get Married

Salvatore wore the Congressional Medal of Honor. His three buddies were killed in a plane crash in Viet Nam. He had been spared. Stephanie was the beautiful girl who would be his bride. They had run out of money and none of the preachers would help them.

They came to me for help. I explained that he would have to be a picture of Christ the Bridegroom and she, a picture of the church. "You will both have to be saved in order to fulfill the picture," I suggested. They both agreed. We knelt at the altar and they received Christ. She was Catholic and after praying the sinner's prayer she crossed herself. It was a bit amusing, but what a blessing to see them get born again!

IV. He Came to the Undertaker's Office

After a funeral sermon for a young girl, I suggested that if many of my congregation were in her place, they would be forever lost. I asked them to consider their ways.

While waiting in the office a young man came in and awkwardly spoke, "I just wanted to tell you that was a good sermon." He just stood there and then spoke again. "Yes, Sir, that was real good," he said. Suddenly, I woke up! "Are you trying to tell me that you want to get saved?" I asked him. "Yes, that's it!" he said. "I want to get right." The boy made a good decision for Christ right on the spot.

V. They Were At the Graveside

The fire had taken both of their small children. "They are both in Heaven," I reminded them, "but you will need to be saved before you can ever see them again."

I waited near the car after the graveside ceremony. The young couple came over to me and said, "We are so glad that our babies are in Heaven. Could you help us get ready, so we can go there someday, too?" They came to church and were baptized. Several people have already been saved through their lives.

VI. Saved by Appointment

He seemed interested. He had come to church three or four times. I called him on the phone and asked, "Can I come to your house on Tuesday at 7:00 p.m. to help you get ready for Heaven?" "Why, er, sure!" he said. "Come on over."

He was waiting for me when I arrived, his Bible in his hand, and in just a moment it was settled. He is one of the bus pastors now, winning souls regularly.

VII. He Built the Pulpit

"I want to do something to help. Could I build the pulpit?" a fellow asked. He did an excellent job. When he delivered it to the church, I asked him, "Are you saved yet?"

"No, not yet," he answered.

"Don't you think a fellow as interested as you ought to be saved?" I asked.

"Yes, Sir," he answered.

It was a matter of minutes before it was settled forever.

VIII. She Was in the Maternity Ward

I visited the new mother with the little baby and explained that, just like this baby being born to get into this life, we would have to be born spiritually to get into the Christian life. She invited Christ in and was born again. She was our church secretary for eleven years.

IX. He Would Be in Hell Now

This is the testimony of our Sunday school superintendent of several years ago. He came home drunk and found a group of us there praying for him. He sneaked around to the back door and I was waiting for him in the kitchen. In a testimony meeting in our church he said, "If it hadn't been for the preacher coming to my house, I would be in Hell right now!"

X. He Thought It Would Be a Good Idea

He was a big man and had a good paying job. His heart attack was a big surprise. He was much better now and wanted to talk about going to Heaven. "What do you think of becoming a Christian?" I asked him. "I think it would be a good idea!" he said. I was glad I went.

XI. Saved in the Barn

"He is out in the barn," his wife told me. I found him and explained why I had come. He listened very attentively, then said, "You mean I can get saved here in the barn?" I assured him he could, and he did!

XII. He Would Not. . .But Did

I had been to the home before. It was the same. "Maybe later, Preacher," he said. Then came the doctor's report. "Your heart is bad; you will have to quit work; you will need heart surgery;

and you may die." I went again and this time it was different. "I guess I had better get it settled, Preacher," he said. And he did! He hasn't died yet—except to self.

XIII. He Planned to Kill Her,
but Got Saved Instead

She was scared and crying when I arrived. She asked the Lord to forgive her for not getting baptized and living right after salvation. Then he came back. He had said he would kill her when he got back. I suggested that maybe we could talk about his troubles. Soon he was sobbing and there on his knees he made peace with God. They were bapized together the next Sunday.

* * *

Surely, the fields are white. People are everywhere. . .and we can win somebody if we try. Every Christian ought to accept a goal and set out to reach at least one a month. Many could win one a week. I won two last night and one today. That is three in less than twenty-four hours. I know of one young fellow who averages one per day and has for the past two years.

What about you? How many will you trust the Lord to give you?

The Devil in the Church

"Put on the whole armour of God, that ye may be able to stand against the wiles of the devil. For we wrestle not against flesh and blood, but against principalities, against powers, against the rulers of the darkness of this world, against spiritual wickedness in high places."—Eph. 6:11,12.

In recent days we have heard much concerning communists hiding in our churches. The National Council of Churches of Christ For America has shouted loud protests and said that it is not so. The American Council of Christian Churches has pointed its finger, like Nathan pointing at David, and declared that anyone with any sense at all could see that it is so. Many well-known members of the National Council of Churches of Christ For America have been known to be card-carrying communists.

Knowing, too, that the strength of any community, state and nation is the character and principle instilled into leaders and workers through the local church, it is only sensible to advocate that one of the chief desires of the communists would be to destroy the Bible-believing church. The communists know that the heart of an individual, as well as his home, which is the primary strength of America, is influenced by his attendance to the house of God. They also know that to openly attack the church would only serve to unify and strengthen it; so, the only other method is to infiltrate and work from within to destroy it.

This does not surprise us, in the least, because this always has been the communist approach. The Devil has been using it for thousands of years. Satan has gotten into our churches and he is succeeding in draining the strength and power. Revival seems to be gone and we are losing ground. More people are being born than being saved. The Devil is stealing our influence, and even our churches are being used against the cause of Christ.

Notice how the church is:

I. FORMAL IN TRADITION

Formalism always has been an enemy of true spirituality. The less power with God a church has, the more ceremony will be involved. This is done to try to cover up for the loss of spiritual power. This is a day of bowing, chanting and reciting meaningless prayers. Men are following procedures, lighting candles and burning incense. There is a trend toward going back to the ceremony of the old Jewish law. Modern churches are complying more every week with the ceremony of the Tabernacle and Temple worship.

We are told, "Therefore by the deeds of the law there shall no flesh be justified in his sight. . ." (Rom. 3:20). In Galatians 3:13 we read, "Christ hath redeemed us from the curse of the law . . . ." Paul tells us in Galatians 5:1: "Stand fast therefore in the liberty wherewith Christ hath made us free, and be not entangled again with the yoke of bondage."

New Testament Christianity is not in keeping ordinances and following regulations laid down by an ecclesiastical headquarters. It is in being led by the Spirit of God. "For as many as are led by the Spirit of God, they are the sons of God" (Rom. 8:14).

Formalism always will expose itself by the following characteristics:

First, it will always be *outward and not inward.* Everything will be done to please people and every decision is made in light of what others will say or do.

Second, it will be *based on law and not love.* Under law men serve God because it is compulsory, but love serves God voluntarily.

Third, it is *for men and not for God.* In the big ecclesiastical meetings across the land, they are deciding and voting on issues to determine whether church members can drink, smoke or get a divorce. Every year the standard comes down to please the sinful heart of man. God's will and plan are not regarded. The plain teaching of the Bible is ignored.

Fourth, it is a *religion of flesh and not spirit.* Galatians 6:8 tells us, "For he that soweth to his flesh shall of the flesh reap corruption; but he that soweth to the Spirit shall of the Spirit reap life everlasting." In other words, they that smoke cigarettes shall, more than likely, get a lung cancer.

Finally, notice that formalism is *all action and no unction.*

Not long ago, I visited a meeting to hear a well-known speaker in a local church. The church was cold and unfriendly. The music had no spirit and the prayer was read instead of prayed. Just as the service started, two little boys in red robes came out and lit candles. At the close they came back and put them out. The messenger exhalted man and emphasized the power of man to overcome his fears and frustrations through doing for and serving others.

At the close of the meeting, no invitation was given for men to repent of sin and turn to God. After the meeting, a social time followed. I was glad to get away, and I do not plan to go again! There is no doubt that Satan is rejoicing in the ministry of this church. They are serving man. There is a lot of action—without the power of God.

Churches are busy with clubs, sales, bakes, projects and all the rest—but, where is the power of God? The words of Jesus need to be heard as found in Matthew 15:3: "Why do ye also transgress the commandment of God by your tradition?"

When a poor needy sinner, with an upset heart, goes to one of these formal churches for help, they quickly recommend that he see a psychiatrist.

Even a sinner, who is blind to God's plan, can see that the Devil is in the church. One man told me that he quit going to church when he was a sinner because the same fellow who poured his liquor and passed his beer to him on Saturday night, was right there in church on Sunday morning to pass him the offering plate. He knew that it wasn't right.

II. FLESHLY TRANSGRESSION

Some think that sin can be sanctified by bringing it into the church. The members of many churches are living sinful, lascivious lives under the cloak of church membership. To them the church is just another club that will help their business or give them more contacts. It seems to be profitable to join the church. A little religion is very convenient at times.

In Galatians 5:16,17 the Word of God declares, "Walk in the Spirit, and ye shall not fulfill the lust of the flesh. For the flesh lusteth against the Spirit, and the Spirit against the flesh. . . ." Again we read, "For he that soweth to his flesh shall of the flesh reap corruption. . . ." (Gal. 6:8). We are encouraged, "But put ye on the Lord Jesus Christ, and make not provision for the flesh, to fulfill the lusts thereof" (Rom. 13:14). Peter tells us, ". . . abstain from fleshly lusts, which war against the soul" (I Pet. 2:11).

The church at Corinth was filled with carnal Christians with problems, strife, divisions, contentions and envies. On the other hand, notice that the church in the Book of Acts was in one accord and unified. When they prayed, great power came and miracles took place. This contrast points out the vast difference between a church led by the Spirit of God and one that the Devil is in.

The church of today is filled with whimpering, jealous, defeated Christians. They are worldly, selfish and cold because they are under the power of the Devil's stress on flesh. Instead of the call of the church, men have given in to the call of the crowd. Instead of love for the Father, it is lust of the flesh. Instead of fishing for men, they are fishing for suckers. They want cocktails, not Christ. Instead of driving the church bus and singing in the choir, they are driving their boats and sipping at their bars. Instead of prayer meeting, they want a party. They are too busy dancing to be a deacon, and they can't be a missionary because they are trying to become a millionaire.

If men would only remember that ". . .greater is he that is in you, than he that is in the world" (I John 4:4).

III. FALSENESS IN TEACHING

Cults and isms have flourished to the extent that thousands have followed the teachings of men. The Devil has cashed in on this. People do not like to be restrained, so they have started religions to suit themselves. Jane Russell was not accepted in the Hollywood Christian group because of a sex picture she made, so she started her own group. Mary Baker Eddy, Joseph Smith, Joseph Russell, Father Devine, Prophet Jones, Campbell, Ellen G. White and many others did not like the restraint of the Bible, so they organized their own groups.

The Bible says, "Be not carried about with divers and strange doctrines. . ." (Heb. 13:9). Again we read, "Beware, lest any man spoil you through philosophy and vain deceit. . ." (Col. 2:8). In Matthew 16:6 we are told, ". . .beware of the leaven of the Pharisees and of the Sadducees."

Many a soul will spend eternity in Hell because of a smooth-talking religious racketeer who loves power and money. The Devil has added influence and power to this campaign against the work of Christ, and thousands of gullible folks have fallen hook, line and sinker for the bait. The Scripture says, "In whom the god of this world hath blinded the minds of them which believe not, lest the light of the glorious gospel of Christ, who is the image of God, should shine unto them" (II Cor. 4:4). Jesus said, "I am the way, the truth, and the life: no man cometh unto the Father, but by me" (John 14:6).

IV. FAILURE IN TEMPTATION

It certainly is not a sin to be tempted by the Devil, but it is a sin to yield. The songwriter has said:

> **Yield not to temptation,**
> **For yielding is sin.**
> **Each vict'ry will help you**
> **Some other to win;**

Fight manfully onward,
Dark passions subdue,
Look ever to Jesus,
He will carry you through.

In the Bible we have the account of many who failed when they were tempted. Eve let God down and disgraced her family. The whole human race has suffered ever since. Lot backslid in Sodom. The temptation to be a big shot got the best of him. His pride and self-esteem caused him to fall into a snare. Achan was tempted and it caused him to steal, bringing judgment on the whole army of Israel. Many died and Achan was exposed and killed. His failure was yielding to temptation.

Solomon gave in to his weakness for women and disobeyed the plain leading of the Lord. David was tempted by flesh, and his lust caused the sin of adultery with Bathsheba, which led to the murder of Uriah. In James 1:14,15, the Word of God states: "But every man is tempted, when he is drawn away of his own lust, and enticed. Then when lust hath conceived, it bringeth forth sin: and sin, when it is finished, bringeth forth death."

But we do not have to fail. The Bible also is filled with examples of men who did not yield in time of trial. Abraham was known as a great man of faith and he was true to God. Joseph was enticed by Potiphar's wife, but he would not yield. Even though he suffered much, he would not disgrace himself. Elijah and Elisha were men who would not give and bow to Baal. Job was subjected to the most horrible fate of all. Daniel was thrown into the lions' den because he would not give in to the modernists.

Finally, see that Christ was tempted in the wilderness. There He was led by the Spirit to be tempted by the Devil. He did not submit to the Devil for a moment, but came out victorious over sin. The Bible says, "There hath no temptation taken you but such as is common to man: but God is faithful, who will not suffer you to be tempted above that ye are able; but will with the temptation also make a way to escape, that ye may be able to bear it" (I Cor. 10:13). Again it says, "My brethren, count it all joy when ye fall into divers temptations" (James 1:1).

We are told in James 1:12, "Blessed is the man that endureth temptation; for when he is tried, he shall receive the crown of life, which the Lord hath promised to them that love him." Peter says, "The Lord knoweth how to deliver the godly out of temptations. . ." (II Pet. 2:9). Solomon warns, "My son, if sinners entice thee, consent thou not" (Prov. 1:10).

In conclusion, let me remind you, dear friend, that the Devil is also after you. He would like to ruin your influence and testimony. Remember that formality, flesh, false teachings and failing Christians are the tools that the Devil uses against God.

The only safeguard is to put on the whole armour of God. If you are not a Christian, open your heart to Christ and be saved right now. Write and tell me about it.

Real Revival

"And the people with one accord gave heed unto those things which Philip spake, hearing and seeing the miracles which he did. For unclean spirits, crying with loud voices, came out of many that were possessed with them: and many taken with palsies, and that were lame, were healed. And there was great joy in that city."—Acts 8:6-8.

There is a vast difference between revival and evangelism. One means awakening of the people of God; the other is a harvesting of souls. Evangelism is the product of revival, and it is the sure result of real revival. When seeking revival, we preach to the saved. When seeking evangelism, we preach to the lost.

Philip saw true revival in Samaria. The people gave heed to his preaching, and accord and unity resulted. Sin and evil began to be dealt with and miracles began to happen. Great joy came upon the people as a final result.

Someone has suggested five facts concerning this revival at Samaria. It was *born* in time of trouble; it *began* with one individual; it *blended* the people together; it *brought out* demons, and it *blessed* everybody. This is the kind of revival we need in our churches. When God sends this kind of revival to us, it will do three necessary things.

First, it will bring about a real sense of the wickedness of sin. Today men do not agree that sin is wicked. Sin is presented as attractive and beautiful by giant billboard signs. The wickedest of sin is passed off as normal, decent behavior. When the morals go down farther and farther, sin is accepted. That which used to be frowned on is welcomed into society. The rattlesnake that once was killed with a hoe is now allowed to curl up on the living room rug.

Old-timers tell us that in their day if you played cards, drank beer or went to the dance you were wicked. But now, if you don't do these things, you are a social misfit. A woman who smoked was looked on as a street woman then; but now, that has all changed.

My friend, it may have changed in the eyes of men, but not in the eyes of God.

Second, it will bring about a right attitude of conversion. Conversion means a change and it needs to be emphasized that this covers every area of our lives. Our social life, family life, business life, personal conduct, habits, language, desires, attitudes and every other phase of our lives should go through a transformation, too, along with our spiritual life. As one converted drunk said to me, "Even the cat knows I've been saved!"

Conversion is not just a decision to clean up and reform ourselves. It is not enough to quit evil and start attending church, reading the Bible, having family and personal prayer etc., etc. There must be genuine repentance and faith which results in the new birth. This is a miracle from God. Anything short of this is not enough.

Third, it will bring about a recognition of our true condition. Many seem to live in a spiritual house of mirrors. They are getting a distorted picture of the real things. We need to look into the true mirror of the Word of God. By plain preaching and seeking the true spirit of revival, we become aware of our failures and sin. Submission and yieldedness is the result of revival. This attitude always results in a true look at ourselves. We need the kind of revival that will stem the tide of sin, put God in His rightful place and accomplish the work of evangelism.

I. REVIVAL THAT WILL STEM
THE TIDE OF SIN

First, we must face the fact of sin's presence. There is no use for us to put our head in a hole like an ostrich. We cannot hide from this truth. We may even try to fool ourselves by covering and hiding the sin from the preacher or our fellow-Christians; but, God sees!

The fact of sin is clearly seen in that the TV is more popular than the church. Our boys and girls know more names of cowboys and ballplayers than they do apostles and Bible characters. The church members stay with the late show until 2:00 a.m., but complain bitterly if it's after 9:00 p.m. when church dismisses. The ball game takes two hours to view and the church only one, but take a vote to see where there is the most interest.

Profanity is more common than witnessing. Those who freely sling God's name around in vileness and profanity are embarrassed if He is mentioned in a reverent way. Thousands curse and swear, while the sacred few tell the good news of redemption to their friends. Cocktail parties are more attractive than prayer meetings. The social drink has been accepted by the church crowd as proper. Some groups have voted that it is proper for the clergy to drink along with their crowd.

Tobacco is a stronger habit than Christlikeness. In spite of the cancer facts and appeal from the American Cancer Society to abstain from the killer weed, the sale in cigarettes, cigars and snuff climbs yearly. Lung cancer, heart trouble and the like brought on by smoking and the increasing number of stillborn babies among smoking mothers, has not slowed things down at all.

Comics are read more than the Bible. The newsstands do not carry the Bible because of a poor volume of sales. Just compare the size of the comic book rack in the five and dime store in any town to the Bible Department. It is made clear what people want.

An evangelist friend of mine, shopping in a Washington D. C. department store, found a small stack of New Testaments priced at $4.25. They had been reduced to $2.13, then to $1.00. Finally, in desperation, they were priced at $.25 each. He bought the whole stack. If this speaks of the spiritual interest of the people of our nation's capital, just where will it all end?

Love and romance stories filled with suggestive sex language, crime books and all the rest have set the pace and trained our youth how to live their lives. Playing cards and card parties have replaced the prayer life. The deck of cards used to be found in the pool hall or the smoky gambler's den, but now they have moved to the respectable living room and the church social hall. Almost all of the community clubs and organizations raise their money now by the gambler's deck.

Feasting has become far more important than fasting. Feeding the spirit and nurturing the life for God has been replaced by the feeding of the flesh. Suppers, bakes, picnics, hot-dog roasts, snacks and teas are the gimmicks now used to get the congregation into the Lord's house.

To sum it all up, living for self has been substituted for living for God. The person who is not aware of the presence of the sin does not have a clean conception of what sin is.

Second, we must face the finality of sin's punishment. Lust leads to sin. ". . .and sin, when it is finished, bringeth forth death" (James 1:15). The social drinker has no intention of ending up in the gutter as a drunk; but, this is where it leads. The billboards do not show the product of their sales.

One young lad spoke the truth when he walked by the downtown bar where a drunk had slumped over on the sidewalk. He opened the barroom door and hollered to the keeper, "Hey, Mister! Your sign fell down."

Necking, dancing and playing with lust seems exciting for the young girl and she never intended for it to go any farther, but later, as prostitute with ruined health and aching heart, she sees that sin has an end. The hardened criminal was not born that way either. No boy or girl who started stealing cookies and sneaking change from Mother's purse intended to get deeper and become a long-term inmate at the penitentiary.

It may not have seemed so bad to be fretful and fussy and even worry a little, but after being labeled a neurotic by the psychologist, we see that it all will catch up to you. When the pastor preached on the family altar, it seemed like such a small matter, but later, during the divorce proceedings and settlements, its importance could be understood.

The untamed sin of lust leads on to gross sin and finally results in a diseased-racked body. One man pitifully summed it all up as he told his story. "Fifteen minutes of pleasure and a lifetime of misery and regret." Paul was right when he said, ". . .whatsoever a man soweth, that shall he also reap" (Gal. 6:7). The ruined reputation is the end. No one would ever believe that it all could happen so fast. The writer of Proverbs says, "A good name is rather to be chosen than great riches. . ." (Prov. 22:1). Abstaining from all appearance of evil is our only sure way to guard our reputation.

Finally, a lost opportunity is the end of carelessness and neglect; we are sure that tomorrow will bring new chances to remedy the situation and do the right thing. But this is not the case. How quickly things happen and opportunities are gone forever. "There is a way which seemeth right unto a man, but the end thereof are the ways of death" (Prov. 14:12)

Third, we can have freedom from sin's power. Men do not have to be dominated by sin. John tells us, "If the Son therefore shall make you free, ye shall be free indeed" (John 8:36). It is not that we reform and untie our hands, nor do we make the key to our shackle. "Jesus paid it all; all to Him I owe. . .," states the songwriter. Paul expressed it, "But thanks be to God, which giveth us the victory through our Lord Jesus Christ" (I Cor. 15:57).

II. REVIVAL THAT WILL PUT GOD IN RIGHTFUL PLACE

God has been humorized and stripped of His glory in the minds of so many, that we have a responsibility to seek for a revival that will bring men to their senses.

First, notice God's rightful place as the Saviour. There is no salvation outside of Christ. Peter said, "Neither is there salvation in any other; for there is none other name under heaven given among men, whereby we must be saved" (Acts 4:12). Jesus said, "I am the way, the truth, and the life: no man cometh unto the Father, but by me" (John 14:6). God was in Christ reconciling the world unto Himself.

Second, notice God's rightful place as sovereign Lord. Revival puts all doubt out of our minds as to who our Lord is. Men are serving self, society, secondary interests and a thousand other gods. . .but God said, "Thou shalt have no other gods before ·me" (Exod. 20:3). Thomas saw it and remarked, "My Lord and my God" (John 20:28). Paul impressed the world with his statement, "Lord, what wilt thou have me to do?" (Acts 9:6).

Third, God is our security. Real revival will bring on a new sense of security like that of Paul in II Timothy 1:12. ". . .for I know whom I have believed, and am persuaded that he is able to keep that which I have committed unto him against that day." John gives us real peace by stating God's position on this. "And I give unto them eternal life; and they shall never perish, neither shall any man pluck them out of my hand" (John 10:28). The words "eternal" and "everlasting" are self-explaining and God used these words to describe our salvation because this is what He meant.

III. REVIVAL THAT WILL ACCOMPLISH THE WORK OF EVANGELISM

The result of the revival of Pentecost was personal evangelism by teams and also Philip and some of the others in campaigns. Jesus came to seek and save that which was lost. This is the closest thing to the heart of God. If we are to please God, we must win the lost to Jesus Christ.

It must be done in the Spirit. The miracle of winning the lost must be accomplished by the miracle power of God. "Not by might, nor by power, but by my spirit, saith the Lord of hosts" (Zech. 4:6). That which is wrought in the flesh is temporal.

It must also be through the Scriptures. We have no authority to advise, counsel and recommend outside of the plain words of God. He has said what He meant. The Word is a sword used by the Spirit to cut down to the heart.

Then, finally, the work must be accomplished by His servants.

God uses men to carry the message to other men. We are exhorted to be fruit-bearers and to produce. We are warned that if we don't produce, there will be inspection and action. Real revival will send us out with our Bibles and in the power of the Spirit to win souls.

May our prayer be that of the psalmist, "Wilt thou not revive us again: that thy people may rejoice in thee?" (Ps. 86:6).

The Holy Guest

"God is a Spirit: and they that worship him must worship him in spirit and in truth."—John 4:24.

The Bible calls the Spirit of God "The Holy Ghost" and "The Holy Spirit"; but, Merv Rosell, preaching a revival in Chattanooga, Tennessee, referred to the Spirit of God as a "Holy Guest." He must be invited in and given liberty as a visitor in the home.

In the Old Testament Scripture we first meet the Holy Spirit in the creation story. God spoke, saying, "Let US make man in our own image." Throughout the Old Testament, we find the Lord appearing to men in many different ways and forms. Sometimes He appeared in the form of fire, then clouds, angels and in many other ways. When the Tabernacle was built in the wilderness the Lord's Presence came in the form of a cloud and He stayed in the Holy of Holies (see Exod. 40:33). The High Priest of Israel went in once a year to offer a sacrifice on behalf of the people.

When the Temple was dedicated by Solomon, again the Lord descended into the Temple and His presence was continually there (see II Chron. 7:1). Because of corruption and outward religious form, the Lord departed from the Temple.

When Jesus was born of the Virgin Mary it was prophesied by Isaiah that He would be called Immanuel, which means, "God with us." John 1:14 states, "And the Word was made flesh, and dwelt among us. . . ." We know that the Lord's Presence was in a human temple, namely, the body of Jesus. Jesus referred to this in John 2:19-21 when talking of the temple of His body. He said, "Destroy this temple and in three days, I will raise it up."

Now, just before Jesus ascended into Heaven after the resurrection, He promised to send the Holy Spirit to the earth. This promise was fulfilled at Pentecost and God, in the form of the Holy Spirit, came again to dwell among men. During the period of grace, or while the Spirit of God is present with us, our bodies are the temple or dwelling place of God (see I Cor. 6:19).

While we are sinners, the Holy Spirit reveals to us our sin, our Saviour and shows us how our sin has been judged on the cross. If we are willing to trust Christ with our soul, He enters our body as a guest at our invitation. As we surrender and yield our body to Him, He gives wisdom, power, peace, etc. This can be seen in a fourfold way: (1) The incoming of the Spirit (Rev. 3:20), (2) The indwelling of the Spirit (I Cor. 3:16), (3) The infilling by the Spirit (Eph. 4:18) and (4) The instruction by the Spirit (I John 2:27).

At the end of the day of grace, when the rapture comes, the Holy Spirit and everybody that He indwells will depart. God will deal with men during the seven years of tribulation that is to follow, just as He did in Old Testament days. After this, God will come and dwell with men for one thousand years in the person of Christ.

Now, in order that we might be more acquainted with the Holy Spirit who lives in our bodies, let me present a threefold study concerning His *PERSONAL ACTIONS, PERSONAL REACTIONS* and His *PERSONAL TRANSACTIONS*.

I. PERSONAL ACTIONS OF OUR HOLY GUEST

1. *HE SPEAKS*. Acts 13:2: ". . .the Holy Ghost said, Separate me Barnabas and Saul for the work whereunto I have called them." He knew exactly who He wanted and what they were to do. When He speaks to us we should be ready to obey.

2. *HE TESTIFIES*. John 15:26: "But when the Comforter is come, whom I will send unto you from the Father, even the Spirit of truth, which proceedeth from the Father, he shall testify of

me." While others testify and advertise themselves and their ideas, activities and programs, the Holy Spirit only presents Jesus Christ.

3. *HE TEACHES*. John 14:26: "But the Comforter, which is the Holy Ghost, whom the Father will send in my name, he shall teach you all things, and bring all things to your remembrance, whatsoever I have said unto you." Who would be more qualified to teach us than one who has God's attributes of omniscience or one who knows all things?

4. *HE GUIDES*. John 16:13: "Howbeit when he, the Spirit of truth, is come, he will guide you into all truth." The Spirit of God knows the answer to all questions and He can see the dangerous places in our pathway. He is familiar with every inch of the trail of life. He is an excellent guide.

5. *HE LEADS*. Romans 8:14: "For as many as are led by the Spirit of God, they are the sons of God." To follow His leading shows great intelligence and spiritual wisdom. We read in Luke, chapter 4, of the account of Jesus' being tempted of the Devil in the wilderness. This story begins with the statement, "And Jesus being full of the Holy Ghost returned from Jordan, and was led by the Spirit into the wilderness." We, too, can come out of our wilderness temptations without sinning, if we will follow as the Spirit leads.

6. *HE SEALS*. Ephesians 4:30: "And grieve not the Holy Spirit of God, whereby ye are sealed unto the day of redemption." The seal signifies God's ownership and protection over us.

7. *HE GIVES GIFTS*. First Corinthians 12:4: "Now there are diversities of gifts, but the same Spirit." These gifts are listed in the following verses as: the gift of wisdom, gift of knowledge, gift of faith, gift of healing, gift of working miracles, gift of prophecy, gift of discerning spirits, gift of divers kinds of tongues and gift of interpretation of tongues. He gives these to whomsoever He will.

8. *HE BAPTIZES*. First Corinthians 12:13: "For by one Spirit are we all baptized into one body, whether we be Jews or Gentiles, whether we be bond or free; and have been all made to

drink into one Spirit." This, of course, refers to spiritual baptism into the body of Christ, and not to water baptism.

9. *HE INTERCEDES.* Romans 8:26: "Likewise the Spirit also helpeth our infirmities: for we know not what we should pray for as we ought: but the Spirit itself maketh groanings which cannot be uttered." How many times we are not able to express what we really mean. How difficult to get across what we have on our hearts. But, when the Spirit intercedes for us, He expresses our heart to the Lord.

10. *HE FORBIDS.* Acts 16:6,7: "Now when they had gone throughout Phrygia and the region of Galatia, and were forbidden of the Holy Ghost to preach the word in Asia, After they were come to Mysia, they assayed to go into Bithynia, but the Spirit suffered them not." It is clear to see that the Holy Spirit is a person with a will. He has the will of the Father and He forbids what is contrary to the will of God. Those who oppose and rebel against His leading are out of God's will for their lives.

11. *HE GIVES LIFE.* John 6:63: "It is the spirit that quickeneth; the flesh profiteth nothing: the words that I speak unto you, they are spirit, and they are life." Man is dead in trespasses and sin, until he is given eternal life, by the Spirit. Spiritual death comes because of Adam's sin; but, resurrection comes by Christ through the Spirit.

12. *HE CONVICTS.* John 16:7,8: "Nevertheless I tell you the truth; It is expedient for you that I go away: for if I go not away, the Comforter will not come unto you; but if I depart, I will send him unto you. And when he is come, he will reprove the world of sin, and of righteousness, and of judgment." Conviction comes as the Spirit points out our sins and points us to Jesus on the cross, judging our sin.

13. *HE COMFORTS.* John 14:26: "But the Comforter, which is the Holy Ghost. . . ." He is also the Comforter in John 15:26 and John 16:7.

14. *HE REGENERATES.* John 3:5: "Jesus answered, Verily, verily, I say unto thee, Except a man be born of water and of the Spirit, he cannot enter into the kingdom of God." To be born of

the Spirit is to be born of God or born from above. This is regeneration or salvation, by the hand of God.

15. *HE EMPOWERS.* Acts 1:8: "But ye shall receive power, after that the Holy Ghost is come upon you: and ye shall be witnesses unto me both in Jerusalem, and in all Judaea, and in Samaria, and unto the uttermost part of the earth."

16. *HE BEARS WITNESS.* Romans 8:16: "The Spirit itself beareth witness with our spirit, that we are the children of God." First John 5:10 tells us, "He that believeth on the Son of God hath the witness in himself. . . ." Assurance and peace about our salvation comes by the Spirit.

II. PERSONAL REACTIONS OF THE HOLY SPIRIT

The Holy Spirit has a personality and a will and can be affected by our actions toward Him. Ways in which He is affected are as follows:

1. *HE CAN BE GRIEVED.* Ephesians 4:30: "And grieve not the holy Spirit of God, whereby ye are sealed unto the day of redemption." To grieve means to go against His desires and injure, harm or hurt Him by resisting, rebelling and spurning His leading. It is for our good and benefit that He acts. When we do not respond, He is grieved.

2. *HE CAN BE VEXED.* Isaiah 63:10: "But they rebelled, and vexed his Holy Spirit: therefore he was turned to be their enemy, and he fought against them." To be vexed means to be grieved, annoyed, angered or agitated. The Spirit will take so much of this and then He will take no more.

3. *HE CAN BE TEMPTED.* Acts 5:9: "How is it that ye have agreed together to tempt the Spirit of the Lord?" Ananias and Sapphira merely twisted the truth around and tried to hide it from the people. They seemed to think that the Holy Spirit would go along with them in the thing, but they were wrong.

4. *HE CAN BE LIED TO.* Acts 5:3: "But Peter said, Ananias, why hath Satan filled thine heart to lie to the Holy Ghost. . .?" Ananias thought his little scheme was well covered and, when he

lied, he considered it a small matter involving man only. Many still feel the same about sinfulness. Little do men realize the seriousness of sinning against God.

5. *HE CAN BE RESISTED.* Acts 7:51: "Ye stiffnecked and uncircumcised in heart and ears, ye do always resist the Holy Ghost: as your fathers did, so do ye." These words of Stephen to the Jews clearly express the true picture of so many today. The Holy Spirit is ready to help, but so often He is resisted.

6. *HE CAN BE QUENCHED.* First Thessalonians 5:19: "Quench not the Spirit." Paul saw that men were restraining and holding back the Spirit. It is a dangerous thing to refuse to give the Spirit His way.

7. *HE CAN BE BLASPHEMED.* Matthew 12:31: "Wherefore I say unto you, All manner of sin and blasphemy shall be forgiven unto men: but the blasphemy against the Holy Spirit shall not be forgiven unto men." It is possible to go too far in resisting the Spirit until He is so offended that He will not attempt to help any further. This can only be done by a non-Christian.

8. *HE WILL WITHDRAW.* Genesis 6:3: "And the Lord said, "My spirit shall not always strive with man. . . ." In the days of Noah, God's Spirit spoke, pleaded and warned men, but finally it was enough and judgment fell. It is still the same today. God's Spirit will only strive with a man so long, then He will depart.

III. PERSONAL TRANSACTIONS OF THE HOLY SPIRIT

There are many cases in the Bible where the presence of the Holy Spirit changed the picture and a great difference came about. Power and authority replaces uncertainty and lack of assurance when the Spirit comes. Listed are some cases of this found in the Bible.

1. *THE SEVENTY ELDERS.* Numbers 11:25: ". . .and it came to pass, that, when the Spirit rested upon them, they prophesied, and did not cease." These men were to help Moses in the job of leading the children of Israel in the wilderness. They

needed God's Spirit and power. What a difference it made to them to have the power of God!

2. *OTHNIEL, THE JUDGE.* Judges 3:10: "And the Spirit of the Lord came upon him, and he judged Israel. . . ." Israel was away from God and the presence of the Holy Spirit helped Othniel judge a backslidden people back to the blessings of God.

3. *GIDEON.* Judges 6:34: "But the Spirit of the Lord came upon Gideon and he blew a trumpet. . . ." God gave this man the power and wisdom to defeat the enemies of Israel through the Holy Spirit.

4. *SAMSON.* Judges 14:6: "And the Spirit of the Lord came mightily upon him, and he rent him as he would have rent a kid, and he had nothing in his hand. . . ." It wasn't Samson who was so strong; it was God's power upon him.

5. *SAUL.* First Samuel 10:10: "And when they came thither to the hill, behold, a company of prophets met him; and the Spirit of God came upon him, and he prophesied among them." Saul was big and strong, but his success was because of God's power. When he lost contact with God, he lost his power.

6. *DAVID.* First Samuel 16:13: "Then Samuel took the horn of oil, and anointed him in the midst of his brethren: and the Spirit of the Lord came upon David from that day forward." David was the kind of person he was because of the Spirit of God being upon him.

7. *SIMEON.* Luke 2:25: ". . .and the Holy Ghost was upon him." Simeon was promised the right to see the Christ. He was waiting patiently and, finally the day came. His desire was filled and he saw the Baby Jesus. He also had the Spirit on him.

8. *PENTECOST.* Acts 2:3: ". . .and it sat upon them." The Holy Spirit came in a great demonstration and sat upon the people. Many were saved as a result of His coming.

9. *CORNELIUS.* Acts 10:44: "While Peter yet spake these words, the Holy Ghost fell on all them which heard the word." Even the Gentiles were given the Spirit.

10. *EPHESIANS.* Acts 19:6: "And when Paul had laid his hands upon them, the Holy Ghost came on them. . . ."

In each of these cases, the coming of the Holy Spirit brought about a change and gave power and authority to the servants of God. It is so necessary today to realized, too, that it is by the Spirit of God that we accomplish things for God.

"More Than Others"

"For if ye love them which love you, what reward have ye? do not even the publicans the same? And if ye salute your brethren only, what do ye more than others? . . ."—Matt. 5:46,47.

In the passages of Scripture just before our text, Jesus is explaining the philosophy of the world. The world says, "If someone does you wrong, pay them back," or "One dirty deed is deserving of another." It has not changed since the time of Christ. Christ is instructing His followers to turn the other cheek, give more than they ask, love enemies and make an impression on the lost world. If they ask you to go a mile, go two miles; and if they want your coat, give them your overcoat, too. In other words, don't leave any room for them to criticize or question your sincerity in serving Christ.

Then, in our text He says that if we are content just to help those who can help us back, we are in the same class with them. We are to do more than others. Our text is a piercing accusation. What are you doing more than others?

In our churches, there are three kinds of people. There are spectators, anticipators and participators. The spectator is just there to observe; the anticipator is expecting real blessings but not doing anything about it, and the participator is busy singing, praying, ushering, planning and doing the work. The participators are the minority, the sacred few who are doing "more than others."

In this same Sermon on the Mount, Jesus said, "Therefore whosoever heareth these sayings of mine, and doeth them, I will liken him unto a wise man, which built his house upon a rock" (Matt. 7:24). James says, "But be ye doers of the word, and not hearers only. . ." (James 1:22).

Someone rightly said, "The church is full of willing folks— those who are willing to work and those who are willing to let them." There is a great need today for the child of God to be willing, concerned, diligent and doing "more than others."

I. OTHERS PUT US TO SHAME

In India, there are men who strip off clothes, cover their naked bodies with white ashes, neither cut nor comb their hair and plaster their heads with cow manure (because the cow is sacred in that country) and endure every type of torture and method imaginable to try to gain the favor of their god.

The Sun Gazer of India sat naked every day for fifteen years gazing at the bright sun, until his eyes were slowly burned out and his limbs withered away from inactivity. He was serving his god in the sun.

The Sadhus of India, who afflict themselves by lying on beds of nails for years, show the same fervency of conviction.

Then, there is the Hindu who held his arms up for twenty years. They soon were stiff from that position, but he illustrates the willingness of others to sacrifice themselves to appease their gods.

The Jehovah's Witnesses, with their strong conviction about blood transfusions, willing to let their children die than go against their ideas, are an example of others putting us to shame.

The Japanese Hell Divers making their suicidal plunge into an enemy ship, only to be blown to bits themselves, tragically illustrates the point. And finally, the communists drive our point home with their bloody oath, "I will kill my own mother before betraying the cause of communism."

God expects us to be zealous, on fire, alive, different, extraordinary, top-caliber and busy doing more than these others who serve the gods of the world. The tragedy is that most Christians are indifferent, backslidden, touchy and living sin-laden lives. The Bible says, "Whatsoever thy hand findeth to do, do it with thy might. . ." (Eccles. 9:10). Again we read, "Whether therefore ye eat, or drink, or whatsoever ye do, do all to the glory of God" (I Cor. 10:31), and also, "Only fear the Lord, and serve him in truth with all your heart: for consider how great things he hath done for you" (I Sam. 12:24).

Is there anyone in your family, church or community who is a better Christian than you are, who reads the Bible more than you do, prays more than you, wins more souls? If so, then shame on you, Christian! Wife, is your husband a better Christian than you? Husband, is your wife a better Christian than you? What do ye more than others?

I believe the Devil still walks to and fro in the earth, as he did in the days of Job. He also has access to Heaven as the accuser of the brethren. When he walks before God to give his report, what embarrassment and shame must come to the Lord because of the sins of His children. Thank God for Job who proved his love by refusing to give in to the Devil! Shame on the many Christians who do not.

I read recently of Vespasion and the forty singing wrestlers. Roman Emperor Nero commanded that all soldiers of his army that claimed Christianity were to be executed. Vespasion, a centurion of this army, received the decree and summoned all his soldiers to appear before him. "Any who cling to the faith of the Christian will be executed," he stated to them. "Now, let him step forward who claims Christ." Instantly the forty wrestlers stepped forward two paces. Vespasion was heartsick and tried to persuade them to denounce their faith.

It was in the dead of winter and he commanded that they be stripped of their clothes and ordered to march out upon a cake of ice in the freezing temperatures. "The fire will be waiting for any who will denounce his false faith," was his parting words.

As they marched away, they sang, "Forty wrestlers, wrestling for Thee, O Christ. . .to win for Thee the victory and for Thee the victor's crown."

All night they sang and Vespasion waited by the fire, until finally near dawn, one frozen, naked soldier crept toward the fire to denounce his Lord. The singing then was heard again.

"Thirty-nine wrestlers, wrestling for Thee, O Christ. . .to win for Thee the victory and for Thee the victor's crown." Vespasion looked out into the darkness and off came his helmet, down went his shield and out into the icy cold went the centurion. The singing could be heard above the whisper of the wind. "Forty wrestlers, wrestling for Thee, O Christ. . .to win for Thee the victory and for Thee the victor's crown."

This is doing "more than others."

II. COMPARING WITH OTHERS

There are many in the church today who are looking around the congregation to pick out the weak and faulty members with which to compare themselves! They seem to be doing a little more than Backslider Ben, Card-Playing Cecil, Double-Living Dan, Gossiping Gertie, Indifferent Ida, Jealous Jenny, Liquor-Drinking Leonard, Movie-Going Molly, Selfish Sally or Worldly Willie, but these are not our standards. We should be looking to Christ and then be made to realize our failures and faults.

In the Bible, Abel did more than Cain, Moses did more than Aaron, Abraham more than Lot, Joseph more than his brethren. Elijah did more than the prophets of Baal, Jacob more than Esau, Job more than his wife, and Peter, James and John did more than the other apostles. "What do ye more than others?"

Men seem to run in ruts and grooves today. They take the line of least resistance. We need some who are willing to be peculiar people and dare to be different from the run-of-the-mill Christians.

Then, there is the problem of excuses. Instead of doing more than others, ". . .they all with one consent began to make excuse" (Luke 14:18). Someone has said, "It is easier to do a thing right than to try to explain why you didn't." The Devil has a bag full of excuses to furnish the Christian who is looking for them, and some of them are not even lies.

Adam blamed Eve when he told the Lord, "The woman whom thou gavest to be with me, she gave me of the tree" (Gen. 3:12). Aaron blamed the people for the golden calf and idol worship while Moses was on the mountain talking to God. He said, "Thou knowest the people, that they are set on mischief" (Exod. 32:22). Then he said, "I cast it into the fire [the gold], and there came out this calf" (Exod. 32:24).

When he had disobeyed God by bringing home the forbidden sheep from Amalek Saul was found out when Samuel came to visit him and heard the bleating of the sheep. Samuel asked, "What meaneth then this bleating of the sheep?" (I Sam. 15:14). Saul tried to excuse his sin by saying, "For the people spared the best of the sheep and of the oxen, to sacrifice unto the Lord thy God" (I Sam. 15:15). Again, Ahab tried to excuse his sin by saying to Elijah, "Art thou he that troubleth Israel?" (I Kings 18:17).

Yes, many are comparing themselves to others and trying to excuse their lack of love and selfish sinning.

III. SOME ARE SATISFIED WITH THEIR STANDING

The greatest sin of Christians today is the sin of giving less than their best. Christians are giving God their leftover time, talents and tithe. This is a day of shallow, surface, superficial Christianity. The standards have been lowered and what was once a disgrace is now accepted as all right. Loose living and shallow standards are bad enough, but to realize that men are content with this state must break the heart of God.

In the home, this trend has had an effect. The old-fashioned family altar has been tossed out for the trash collector; discipline of children has been replaced by modern psychological methods; beer in the icebox, cigarettes in the shirt pockets of teenage boys and in the purses of teenage girls is considered smart; lewd, filthy magazines in the book racks, and the influence of crime, alcohol, sex, etc., on TV is now part of acceptable living.

In the average community, we see it again. Clubs and organizations are sponsoring parties and dancing that encourage drinking and lowering of morals, and they refuse to stand against sin and corruption. As the rattlesnake creeps toward the small child and the old-fashioned preacher starts to kill it with a stick, the community cries, "Thou shalt not kill."

In the church, not much better things can be said. The advance of modern and liberal theology has frowned on standards of separation and godliness. The Sunday school tables have been pushed back into the corner to make room to dance. The altar has been removed and a bar put in the social hall; turkey bazaars, rummage sales and selling chances on cars have taken the place of tithing; movie and book reviews and talks on current events have replaced the sermons on sin and salvation; the opera and classical music has bid good-bye to "Amazing Grace," "Power in the Blood" and "At Calvary."

Then, the individual Christian seems satisfied just as he is. The average Christian is worldly, selfish and unfaithful—living a life of prayerlessness and having no power. At the Judgment Seat of Christ, where every Christian will give an account of deeds done in the body, we will see what we have done "more than others." Our work shall be tried by fire and those who have built with wood, hay and stubble shall suffer loss of reward.

Christian, now is the time to seek to do "more than others" by building with gold, silver and precious stones.

Finally, the lost man seems satisfied with his standing. He is sure that the Lord will open the doors of Heaven and allow him to come in. Remember, friend, "Except ye repent, ye shall all likewise perish" (Luke 13:3) and "Except a man be born again, he cannot see the kingdom of God" (John 3:3).

The Lord is coming to take us soon and there is no time for delay. Those who would change their standing before they stand before God, will need to get to it! Will you, my friend, surrender to Christ and His will for your life?

Measuring Your Faith

". . .According to your faith be it unto you."—Matt. 9:29.

These tremendous words were spoken by Jesus to two blind men. They were greatly rewarded by their faith because their eyes were opened.

In one of his sermons, Dr. Vance Havner points out that Jesus did not say, according to your "fate" or according to your "fortune"; nor did He say, according to your "fame," "friends" or "feelings," but He did say, "According to your faith. . ." (Matt. 9:29).

There are five different kinds of faith affecting our lives.

1. *NATURAL FAITH.* This is faith in a bank where money will be safe, faith in a mailbox that our letter will be delivered, or faith in an employer that we will be paid at the end of the week.

2. *INTELLECTUAL FAITH.* A woman baking a cake and following a recipe is exercising intellectual faith. She believes that the cake will result from pouring in certain ingredients.

Recently, we had an eclipse of the sun. Scientific facts led us to accept by faith that the eclipse would come at a certain time and none of us were disappointed, as it came right on schedule. The next one is scheduled to come in 2024 and all of us believe that it will be on schedule, too.

3. *HISTORICAL FAITH.* We believe that Napoleon actually lived and marshalled a great army. We believe that George Washington was the first President of the United States and that

Abraham Lincoln gave the Gettysburg Address. This is historical faith.

4. *SAVING FATH*. This is Bible faith that God will keep His promise and save us by grace, through faith.

5. *VICTORIOUS FAITH*. This is the faith of a child of God that helps him to exercise prayer and obedience in the Christian life, believing that God will give certain rewards and benefits because He has promised to do so. We read in the Scriptures, "And this is the victory that overcometh the world, even our faith" (I John 5:4).

In this message we are not discussing natural faith, intellectual faith, historical faith or saving faith; but let us consider victorious faith that helps the Christian to do things for God.

I. DEGREES OF FAITH

The Bible speaks of a "measure of faith" and also of a "proportion of faith." Our text speaks of the term, "According to your faith." This seems to indicate that there are various degrees of faith. Let us consider several verses that help us to understand this truth.

1. *NO FAITH*. In the Bible, we read the statement, "How is it that ye have no faith?" (Mark 4:40). Jesus asked this question of His disciples in the boat when they feared that they would perish. Surely there are many defeated Christians living without power and victory who have no faith.

2. *LITTLE FAITH*. In Matthew 8:26 Jesus said, "O ye of little faith." This again is the account of the disciples in the ship.

3. *WEAK FAITH*. "Him that is weak in the faith receive ye . . ." (Rom. 14:1). Here the Apostle Paul is referring to an immature Christian who has not been made strong yet. He is spoken of as being weak in the faith.

4. *DEAD FAITH*. We read, "Even so faith, if it hath not works, is dead" (James 2:17). Genuine faith brings forth action. There is proof when there is faith. James admonished his readers to show him their faith by their works.

5. *VAIN FAITH*. The Bible speaks again of another kind of faith. ". . .and your faith is also vain" (I Cor. 15:14). The word "vain" means empty or of no avail.

6. *GREAT FAITH*. Jesus spoke to the Gentile woman who sought for crumbs from under the table and said to her, "I say unto you, I have not found so great faith, no, not in Israel" (Luke 7:9). In several places Jesus spoke of those who had great faith.

7. *FULL OF FAITH*. The Bible says this of Barnabas: "For he was a good man, and full of the Holy Ghost and of faith" (Acts 11:24). This early New Testament Christian was a tremendous example and pattern for all believers. What a great compliment, that he was full of faith!

8. *STEADFAST FAITH*. ". . .beholding your order, and the steadfastness of your faith in Christ" (Col. 2:5). There is great peace and contentment in being settled and relaxed about the promises of God. Israel continued in doubt and unbelief, but Paul complimented the early Christians because of their steadfastness of faith.

9. *RICH IN FAITH*. James speaks in his book of being rich in faith. "Hath not God chosen the poor of this world rich in faith?" (James 2:5). He is insinuating that faith is a more valuable asset than money.

10. *PRECIOUS FAITH*. Peter wrote, ". . .to them that have obtained like precious faith. . ." (II Pet. 1:1). He was referring, of course, to our salvation that makes us partakers of the grace and mercy of God. This is surely a precious attribute. The word "precious" is often used in relation to something that is scarce and very valuable, such as precious stones; but here, it is "precious faith."

11. *HOLY FAITH*. Then the Bible speaks finally of "holy faith." ". . .building up yourselves on your most holy faith. . ." (Jude 20).

In all of these Bible phrases, we see an evidence of degrees of faith.

II. MEN OF FAITH

No sermon on faith would be complete without reference to Hebrews, chapter 11, where we find the great Hall of Fame. God's men of faith are listed one by one, with comment about their ministries and achievements. We read about:

1. *ABEL*. "By faith Abel. . ." (11:4). We read how Abel was able to offer up a more excellent sacrifice than his brother Cain because he saw with the eye of faith that his act of slaying a lamb was a symbol of the sacrifice of Christ on the cross.

2. *ENOCH*. "By faith, Enoch was translated that he should not see death" (11:5). It is said that Enoch walked with God. His walk was inspired by his confidence in the words of God. He was surely a man of faith.

3. *NOAH*. "By faith Noah. . .prepared an ark to the saving of his house. . ." (11:7). God had said it was going to rain. No one else believed, but Noah had great confidence in God's promise and rain it did, forty days and nights. Noah was glad he had faith and all of the others wished they had!

4. *ABRAHAM*. "By faith Abraham, when he was called to go out. . .went out, not knowing wither he went" (11:8). Abraham's faith led him into a land that he had not seen. In fact, he did not know where he was going! He was simply following God's leadership, trusting that the Lord would keep His promise to make his seed as the sand of the sea and the stars of the sky and the dust of the earth.

5. *SARA*. We also read of Sara's faith. "Through faith also Sara herself received strength to conceive seed, and was delivered of a child when she was past age" (11:11). It is said that by faith Sara delivered a child when she was past the age of bearing.

6. *ISAAC*. It was faith that caused Isaac to put the blessing on Jacob and also on Easu (see 11:20). He actually believed that his prophecy would be carried out in the lives of the two young men.

7. *JACOB*. "By faith Joseph, when he was a dying, blessed both the sons of Joseph" (11:21). He blessed Manasseh and

Ephraim, and promised that certain things would come to pass in their lives. God had promised this to Jacob openly and publicly, declaring that it would come to pass.

8. *MOSES.* It was faith that caused Moses to turn down all that was offered as the son of Pharaoh's daughter (11:24). He chose to go with God's people and suffer their afflictions, because he believed this was God's will.

9. *JOSHUA.* It was by faith that Joshua was helped to see the walls of Jericho fall. God had committed Himself to Joshua and promised that it would come to pass. Joshua led his people to the city of Jericho, trusting the Lord would bring it to pass. They would have surely branded him a nut and a fool had it not happened as it did. But, Joshua was willing to take his chances and bank on the promises of God.

10. *RAHAB.* Rahab, inside the city, also worked by faith (see 11:31). It brought about the saving of her household.

The Bible is filled with stories of men of faith who believed God.

III. QUESTIONS ABOUT FAITH

1. *WHAT IS FAITH?* The Bible says, "Now faith is the substance of things hoped for, the evidence of things not seen" (Heb. 11:1).

2. *WHERE DO WE GET FAITH?* "So then, faith cometh by hearing and hearing by the word of God" (Rom. 10:17). The more a person reads the Bible and meditates in the Book, the more he will have. The Bible promises, "For whosoever shall call upon the name of the Lord shall be saved" (Rom. 10:13). But the next verse explains further, "How then shall they call on him in whom they have not believed? and how shall they believe in him of whom they have not heard?" (vs. 14).

3. *WHAT DOES FAITH DO FOR A SINNER?* Faith brings salvation to the sinner. "For by grace are ye saved through faith . . ." (Eph. 2:8). The thief on the cross is an example of this. He had no opportunity to make restitution or even to be baptized.

He simply trusted in Christ and went that day to Paradise.

4. *WHAT DOES FAITH DO FOR THE SAINT?* For the Christian, faith is the overcoming factor. We read, "And this is the victory that overcometh the world, even our faith" (I John 5:4). Christians of great faith do great works and accomplish great things for God.

5. *WHAT CAN WE DO BY FAITH?* In the Scriptures we read that it is possible to "walk by faith," "pray in faith," "add to your faith," "contend for the faith," "continue in the faith" and many other such phrases.

6. *WHAT SHOULD WE NOT DO?* We read in the Bible that it is possible to "depart from the faith," "deny the faith," "err from the faith" and "waver in faith." These things are to be avoided.

Someone has said that faith "sees the invisible, faith tries the impossible and faith bears the intolerable." Surely faith is a great characteristic in the life of a human being. We should pray as the disciples, "Lord, I believe; help thou mine unbelief" (Mark 9:24).

Several years ago I was visiting in South Detroit and one of the men in the church took me on a tour of an atomic energy plant. He showed me in the control room thousands of gauges, computers, little red and green clicking lights, thermostats, etc. That big room looked like the cockpit of a jet plane multiplied several dozen times.

In the process of the tour, he showed me a little red button and explained that, if one pushed that button down, everything stopped working. The nuclear reactor would stop putting out atomic energy and shut down the flow of molten liquid that created steam, turning the turbines that made electricity for the city of Detroit. To pull the little red button up made everything begin to click, buzz and purr.

He said, "Do you know what that little red button represents to me?" Of course, I did not know what he was getting at. Then, with a sparkle in his eye, he said, "That button is faith." He explained that, when faith is turned on, it opens up a brand new world. It makes Heaven real, the presence of God sure and the promises of the Bible definite and specific. Without faith, everything is dead, dark and gloomy.

Lord, help us to believe.

Grasping for More

"Thou shalt not covet thy neighbour's house, thou shalt not covet thy neighbour's wife, nor his manservant, nor his maidservant, nor his ox, nor his ass, nor any thing that is thy neighbour's."—Exod. 20:17.

Our world is plagued with many curses. Among its worst is covetousness. In the Ten Commandments, God strictly forbids this inner sin. He calls it sin to covet a neighbor's house, wife, servants, oxen, donkeys or anything else that a neighbor might have. The dictionary definition of "covetousness" is "grasping for more." Another definition is "greedy of gain." This is the sin of selfishness. Dr. Lee Roberson calls this, "An ancient sin dogging the steps of modern man."

A story is told of a peasant who murmured to a giant landholder of the unfairness of it all. Knowing the nature of men, the landholder promised to give the peasant all the land he could walk around in a whole day. The peasant, greedily trying to take in all the area possible, overexerted himself and dropped with a heart attack and died. He ended up with nothing.

I would like for us to notice three things about covetousness: the SIN of covetousness, the SOURCE of covetousness and the SORROW of covetousness.

I. THE SIN OF COVETOUSNESS:
(What Is It?)

In the first chapter of Romans, Paul tells us that the wrath of God is revealed from Heaven against all ungodliness and unrighteousness. He tells us that men are filled with all manner of wickedness and corruption. Among the many foul sins listed, covetousness is near the top.

Achan, the man who brought judgment upon Joshua's army, committed this sin. The Lord told Joshua to destroy Jericho after the walls fell down flat. He warned him that all the gold, all the silver and all the spoils of battle were His. Achan saw the wedge of gold, the 200 shekels of silver and the goodly Babylonian garments. He began to covet them and he took them. He stole the "accursed thing" (see Josh. 7:15). Achan could not help what he saw, but he could help what he coveted and what he stole.

The outcome of this story is one of the saddest in the Bible: "And all Israel stoned him with stones, and burned them with fire, after they had stoned them with stones" (Josh. 7:25).

There is also the story in Luke's Gospel of two fellows who were fighting each other over an inheritance. Jesus said, "Take heed, and beware of covetousness, for a man's life consisteth not in the abundance of the things which he possesseth" (Luke 12:15). Jesus then told of the rich man who talked about "my fruits," "my barns," "my goods," and "my soul" (see Luke 12). Instead of putting his great wealth to work, he intended to build great storehouses to store his goods and hoard it for himself. Jesus said, "Thou fool, this night thy soul shall be required of thee" (Luke 12:20).

Covetousness causes unhappiness and misery. Satisfaction never comes until this greedy sin is crushed. Covetousness also causes people to steal from God. Achan is not the only person to steal God's gold and silver. Every week thousands of Christians receive God's blessings and wages; then, when He asks for ten percent back, they ignore His command and turn a deaf ear.

Covetousness causes people to pass up opportunities to do great things for God. Those who could sponsor missionaries, buy buses, help build buildings and a thousand other pressing things are busy piling it up higher. The opportunities are lost and then comes the grave and the judgment.

A Kansas peddler living in poverty insisted that he was not

able to pay a $5.00 debt. A few days later he was found dead of malnutrition. Investigators were looking through his possessions and found $61,000 in cash and bonds. The state got it all. This story is repeated hundreds of times each year.

II. THE SOURCE OF COVETOUSNESS:
(Where Does It Come From?)

Jesus said, "For from within, out of the heart of men, proceed evil thoughts, adulteries, fornication, murders, thefts, covetousness. . ." (Mark 7:21,22).

Ezekiel cried out, "And they come unto thee as thy people cometh, and they sit before thee as my people, and they hear thy words, but they will not do them: for with their mouth they shew much love, but their heart goeth after their covetousness" (Ezek. 33:31).

Ahab, the wicked king of Israel, one day saw Naboth's vineyard. He coveted it and approached Naboth about selling it. Because it was an inheritance, it could not be sold. Ahab pouted and sulked until Jezebel, the wicked-hearted queen, cooked up a scheme to have Naboth killed. The moment he was dead, Ahab rose up and took possession of Naboth's vineyard. His covetousness led to stealing and murder. Elijah came to the vineyard and announced to Ahab, "In the place where dogs licked the blood of Naboth shall dogs lick thy blood, even thine" (I Kings 21:19).

There are still a lot of Ahabs around, but their sin will find them out, also.

> He said that he would retire
> When he had made a million clear
> And so he toiled into the dusk
> From day to day and year to year.
>
> At last, he put his ledgers up
> And laid the stock reports aside
> But when he started out to live,
> He found he had already died.

III. THE SORROW OF COVETOUSNESS:
(Where Does It Lead?)

The stories of Achan, Ahab and the rich man all end in sorrow. The Apostle Paul declared, "For the love of money is the root of all evil: which while some coveted after, they have erred from the faith, and pierced themselves through with many sorrows" (I Tim. 6:10).

A successful businessman and his friends were talking and laughing together and enjoying success. The businessman told of his childhood of poverty. Someone had given him a big coin. To have a coin was rare for children then, and his little sister begged to hold it. He laughed over the memory of all the chores he could get her to do for him just to get to hold the coin. He told of a day when she minded the cows all day for the privilege of holding the coin, only to have to give it up at the end of the day. All of the men laughed again at the childishness of the sister.

Just then, one man not laughing, reminded the businessman that all he was doing now in labor and service was for the privilege of holding on to a few possessions. "The end of the day is coming and you will have to give them up like your little sister did."

My reader friend, that is exactly how it is with all of us. Jesus warned, "Lay not up for yourselves treasures upon earth, where moth and rust doth corrupt, and where thieves break through and steal: But lay up for yourselves treasures in Heaven. . ." (Matt. 6:19,20).

How many there are today who are destroying their very life through covetousness. How many more are destroying even their soul for the same reason. Then, thousands of thousands are ruining the lives of their family and friends as they grasp for more. "Thou shalt not covet" (Exod. 20:17).

In the Bible we read, "Mortify therefore your members which are upon the earth. . .covetousness" (Col. 3:5). Again we read, "Let your conversation be without covetousness. . ." (Heb. 13:5). The Bible warns, "But fornication, and all uncleanness, or covetousness, let it not be once named among you" (Eph. 5:3). Then we read the words, "Beware of covetousness, for a man's life consisteth not in the abundance of the things which he possesseth" (Luke 12:15).

Listen today to Jesus: "But seek ye first the kingdom of God, and his righteousness; and all these things shall be added unto you" (Matt. 6:33).

Now, there is only one area where the Bible encourages us to covet. It says, "But covet earnestly the best gifts" (I Cor. 12:31). We are to look around us and see faithfulness, loyalty, dependability, love and other good things in the lives of Christians and covet those things. We should grasp, desire and seek after the fruits of the Spirit and not after the earthly possessions that belong to our neighbor.

Great Things Happen
When We Pray

"Call unto me, and I will answer thee, and shew thee great and mighty things, which thou knowest not."—Jer. 33:3.

Moses cried out to God and God spared Israel from judgment. Joshua's prayer made the sun stand still. Hannah's prayer was answered with a baby boy. Solomon got wisdom in answer to his prayer. Fire came down from Heaven when Elijah prayed and devoured the sacrifice on Mount Carmel. Jonah's prayer brought him out of the belly of the whale. Elijah had the great power of God upon his life. But when Elisha prayed for a double portion of the Spirit, God did not bat an eye when He gave it to him.

Ten lepers prayed and were instantaneously healed. Peter prayed and Dorcas arose from the dead. The thief on the cross prayed and was saved immediately. The early church prayed, and the place was shaken where they were gathered togther. Peter got out of jail in answer to the early Christians' prayers. The door of the Philippian jail fell off when Paul and Silas prayed. It is fascinating to read of the accounts of the prayers of the saints of God in the Bible.

Church history books will stir up your soul, too, as you read how God answered the prayers of George Mueller of Bristol and David Brainerd of New England. J. Hudson Taylor and Charles Finney believed the Bible and got the power of God through answered prayer. They called upon God and He answered them and showed them great and mighty things which they knew not.

It was Abraham Lincoln who said, "Many times I have been forced to my knees, realizing there was simply no other place to go." George Washington met the crisis of Valley Forge on his knees in prayer. In a speech to the Constitutional Convention, Benjamin Franklin reminded the delegates of the daily prayer to God for the guidance and protection that they had offered. Stonewall Jackson said, "I have so fixed the habit in my mind that I never raise a glass of water to my lips without lifting my heart to God in thanks and prayer for the Water of Life."

The Bible is filled with promises to modern-day Christians, and God still promises to hear and answer prayer.

We read in John 14:13,14, "And whatsoever ye shall ask in my name, that will I do, that the Father may be glorified in the Son. If ye shall ask any thing in my name, I will do it."

John 15:7 says, "If ye abide in me, and my words abide in you, ye shall ask what ye will, and it shall be done unto you."

First John 3:22 reads, "And whatsoever we ask, we receive of him, because we keep his commandments, and do those things that are pleasing in his sight."

First John 5:14, 15 tells us, "And this is the confidence that we have in him, that, if we ask any thing according to his will, he heareth us: And if we know that he hears us, whatsoever we ask, we know that we have the petitions that we desired of him."

Matthew 7:7 reads, "Ask, and it shall be given you; seek, and ye shall find; knock, and it shall be opened unto you."

In Matthew 21:22 we read, "And all things, whatsoever ye shall ask in prayer, believing, ye shall receive."

James 5:16 says, "The effectual fervent prayer of a righteous man availeth much."

In James 4:2 we are told, "Ye have not, because ye ask not." Clyde Gray said,

> Oh gracious Lord in Heaven,
>   You sit upon your throne.
> I can't send You a letter,
>   Or call You upon the phone
> To thank You for the blessings
>   You have given me each day.

> Lord, there have been so many,
>   In every precious way.
> I can't send You a message
>   By missile through the air.
> The only way I am sure of,
>   Dear Lord, is by prayer.

1. *People in Trouble Ought to Pray.* The psalmist said, "This poor man cried, and the Lord heard him, and saved him out of all his troubles" (Ps. 34:6).

2. *People Who Need Wisdom Ought to Pray.* "If any of you lack wisdom, let him ask of God, that giveth to all men liberally, and upbraideth not; and it shall be given him" (James 1:5).

3. *People Who Need Power Ought to Pray.* Jesus said, "If a son shall ask bread of any of you that is a father, will he give him a stone? Or if he ask a fish, will he for a fish give him a serpent? Or if he shall ask an egg, will he offer him a scorpion. If ye then, being evil, know how to give good gifts unto your children: how much more shall your heavenly Father give the Holy Spirit to them that ask him?" (Luke 11:11-13).

4. *People Who Want Revival Ought to Pray.* "If my people, which are called by my name, shall humble themselves, and pray, and seek my face, and turn from their wicked ways; then will I hear from heaven, and will forgive their sin, and will heal their land" (II Chron. 7:14).

5. *People Who Want Cleansing Ought to Pray.* David prayed, "Search me, O God, and know my heart: try me, and know my thoughts: And see if there be any wicked way in me, and lead me in the way everlasting" (Ps. 139:23,24).

6. *People Who Want to Know God's Way Ought to Pray.* Moses prayed, "Now therefore, I pray thee, if I have found grace in thy sight, shew me now thy way, that I may know thee, that I may find grace in thy sight: and consider that this nation is thy people" (Exod. 33:13).

7. *People Who Want to Be Saved Ought to Pray.* Peter cried out, "Lord, save me" (Matt. 14:30). The Apostle Paul admonished us to "Pray without ceasing" (I Thess. 5:17). Jesus

said, "Men ought always to pray, and not to faint" (Luke 18:1).

Someone has said, "God waits to do the will of praying men." Remember that prayer is the Christian's greatest privilege. It is his greatest tool, his greatest weapon and his greatest opportunity. It is the key to God's storehouse, the switch to God's power station and the greatest work in which one can become involved.

May all of us say, with Samuel, "God forbid that I should sin against the Lord in ceasing to pray for you" (I Sam. 12:23).

The Drama of Human Struggle

"In all this Job sinned not, nor charged God foolishly."—Job 1:22.

The story of Job is a great classic in human struggle. Why people suffer is a question that men have been asking since the Garden of Eden. Whether it is a locust trying to free itself of its shell after seventeen years in the ground, or a baby chick trying to get out of an egg, or a butterfly coming out of a cocoon, or a baby being born into this life, the lesson that life begins with a struggle is well-emphasized. Truly, this is just the beginning of the struggle, for it continues from the cradle to the grave.

But through struggle, travail and labor comes birth; and so, testing and temptation deliver us to maturity and blessedness. When the winds of persecution blow on the oak tree it sends down roots deeper and deeper to maintain the giant tree in its full growth. We must remember that experience and involvement are the best teachers. Musicians come from practice, drill and hours of labor, not from theory. Good farmers have gone to the plow handles, not agricultural books.

Some men know that God answers prayer and provides for His own from firsthand experience; to others it is hearsay and secondhand faith.

When Abraham says, "The Lord will provide," everybody believes him.

When Daniel says, "The Lord will deliver you," no one argues.

When the three Hebrew children say, "God cares for His own," everybody shouts, "Amen"!

When Paul and Silas say, "You don't have to stay in jail if you know how to pray," everybody has to agree.

So, there is a purpose in experiences and struggles. We learn to prove God that we might glorify Him with our own mouths.

The test of a man is the fight that he makes, the grip that he duly shows, the way that he stands on his feet and takes life's numerous bumps and blows. In all of it God is working to conform us to the image of His Son. This is what the Bible means when it says, "Let us go on unto perfection" (Heb. 6:1).

Now, the story of Job is the greatest example of this in the Bible. Let us notice the seven great tests of Job's life.

I. The Test of Prosperity

Job was wealthy and most people have trouble with this. His wealth made him important. He was considered the greatest man in the East. But with all of this Job remained humble, thoughtful and he worshiped God. So very few can take the test of prosperity.

Mr. Hart Danks wrote the great song, "Silver Threads Among the Gold," and dedicated it to his wife. It was a masterpiece! Royalties began to roll in, dissention followed the quick, easy money and separation resulted. He was found dead with a piece of paper in his hand which read: "It is hard to grow old alone."

Disagreements arose between the widow and children over the royalties. She lived alone for many years, then died in a lodging house. The song that brought comfort to millions of aging hearts, brought riches to the Danks' home, but with prosperity came grief. When riches entered peace and happiness fled, ruined by prosperity.

Let us remember:

"But they that will be rich fall into temptation and a snare, and into many foolish and hurtful lusts, which drown men in destruction and perdition. For the love of money is the root of all evil: which while some coveted after, they have erred from the faith, and pierced themselves through with many sorrows."—I Tim. 6:9,10.

> Dug from the mountainside,
>   Washed in the glen,
> Servant am I, or the master of men.
> Steal me, I curse you,
>   Earn me, I bless you,
> Grasp me and hoard me,
>   A friend shall possess you.
> Lie for me, die for me,
>   Covet me, take me, Angel or Devil
> I am what you make me—money.

II. The Test of Adversity

Job lost his money. The servants came one by one announcing the great losses. Storms, hail, fire, drought and sickness destroys our pile. Again and again the crash comes.

One man confided in a preacher friend that he had lost everything in the Stock Market crash. "I am sorry to hear that your wife has died," said the preacher.

"Oh, my wife is not dead," declared the man.

The preacher replied, "I thought you said you lost everything. I am sorry your children are all gone."

"My children are all well," he said to the preacher.

"Well," the preacher said, "I am sorry you lost your health."

"There is nothing wrong with my health," he said.

The preacher then remarked, "I am sorry that all of your friends have forsaken you."

"But," said the man, "my friends have not gone anywhere."

"But you told me that you lost everything," said the kind preacher. "It seems that the only thing that you have lost is money. You still have the great and valuable things of life."

The man realized his mistake and corrected his thinking.

III. The Test of Sorrow

Job lost all of his children. He was an affectionate, considerate father. This loss was greater sorrow than all of his property. On three different occasions I have seen two caskets out of the same family. One time two beautiful teenage girls had eaten something that killed them. Another occasion was where two little children were burned in a fire. Another was when a father and daughter had drowned while swimming. These were doubly sad.

But in Job's case, there were ten caskets in one day. This surely was the unspeakable test of sorrow. Job surely could sing with the old blacks of the South, "Nobody knows the trouble I've seen." But, praise God, He stayed true and stood faithful!

IV. The Test of Physical Affliction

Job was stricken with boils from the crown of his head to the soles of his feet. He moved out of his house and abode in a pile of ashes, and scraped the corruption from his sores with a piece of potsherd. Job did not complain. He suffered quietly.

I have just come from the funeral home after burying a man who had been in our hospital, I suppose, a dozen times. Sometimes he'd been there for as much as two and three weeks at a time. I never knew a person to suffer any more than he did. Yet, I never heard him complain. He reminded me of the story of Job.

It is possible to commit our way unto the Lord and trust in Him. God promises grace sufficient for our hour of need. How we need to learn the lesson of physical affliction.

V. Job Was Tested by the Betrayal of His Wife

When the world has been cruel, at least a man can go home. One of the best things a man has, after a day of misunderstanding or a time of burden or social pressure, is the sympathy of his family. But now, this was gone too. This was the bitterest of all. Mrs. Job had, undoubtedly, enjoyed the prosperity of her husband. She had not stood with him in adversity and sorrow. She was bitter and mad at God. In the time when he needed her most, she failed him. A woman can be the dearest thing a man has in the world, or the meanest. Her words had teeth. They cut like a knife and stung like the bite of a viper. Her hissing words came forth, "Curse God and die" (Job 2:9). She was calling Job a fool, but Job held steady. God gave him patience. What a blessing that Job did not lash back at her. Rather he held his tongue and, I think, prayed for grace.

VI. The Test of Doubt

Job was an educated man. We believe he was an intellectual. I suppose the greatest test was to try to explain all of this away by circumstance and luck. The wise men came and tried to persuade Job that no God could be in back of all his troubles. They gave convincing arguments that would have been enough to shake the ordinary man off his foundation. They called him unreasonable. But Job said, "For I know that my redeemer liveth, and that he shall stand at the latter day upon the earth: And though after my skin worms destroy this body, yet in my flesh shall I see God" (Job 19:25,26).

VII. Job Endured the Spiritual Test

The apparent abandonment of God seemed to seal the whole matter. The sorrows fell like rain, and trouble came like a swarm of bees. The crosses were piled on Job's back. His path was strewn with thorns. His days were full of toil and his nights were sleepless. He could have cried out with Christ, "My God, my God, why hast thou forsaken me?" (Mark 15:34). Rather, he cried, "Oh, that I knew where I might find him! That I might come even to his seat! I would order my cause before him, and fill my mouth with arguments. I would know the words which he would answer me, and understand what he would say unto me" (Job 23:3-5).

Job had a Red Sea before him, mountains on either side, and a host of Pharaoh's army crashing down upon him. He was in the lions' den, the fiery furnace and on the cross.

Someone might ask, "When we get in Job's shoes, does Jesus care?" The answer,

> O yes, He cares, I know He cares,
> His heart is touched with my grief;
> When days are weary, the long nights dreary,
> I know my Saviour cares.

Finally Job said, "But he knoweth the way that I take; when he hath tried me, I shall come forth as gold" (Job 23:10). He prayed with Jesus, "O my Father, if it be possible, let this cup pass from me: nevertheless not as I will, but as thou wilt" (Matt. 26:39). When the troubles and trials of life come rolling like waves on the beach, may we say with Job, "Though he slay me, yet will I trust in him. . ." (Job 13:15).

Halfway Boulevard

"But none of these things move me, neither count I my life dear unto myself, so that I might finish my course with joy, and the ministry, which I have received of the Lord Jesus, to testify the gospel of the grace of God."—Acts 20:24.

". . .I have finished my course. . . ."—II Tim. 4:7.

Recently I was driving back toward the city of Hagerstown, Maryland, on Interstate 70 and there, in big white letters on a green background, were the words, "HALFWAY BOULEVARD." Pastor Homer Boese and I were returning from dinner and a visit to the home of Rev. and Mrs. Tyler May of Hancock, Maryland. I remarked to Homer, "That's the street most Christians live on." He quickly agreed.

In our text, we find a man who was not satisfied to live there. He was not happy on twelve-mile road, four-mile road, or even one-mile out. He had to be right in the heart of things for God. Paul is saying to us, "I don't care if they criticize me, beat me, lock me up in jail, stone me and finally kill me: I want to be an all-out, dedicated Christian. I want to finish my course."

Paul Was Not Ashamed of the Gospel. He was always glad to be identified with Christ. He stated on one occasion, "For I am not ashamed of the gospel of Christ; for it is the power of God unto salvation to every one that believeth; to the Jew first, and also to the Greek" (Rom. 1:16).

An evangelist came to our church one time and asked folks to give a testimony. Several did. Then he asked if any of the Devil's children wanted to give a testimony for him. Nobody moved.

Down on the street, in the taprooms and on the street corners, men seem to be willing to speak out for sin and all the rest that the Devil stands for. Yet around the church they are quiet as mice. I'm afraid that is also true in reverse. The children of God are afraid to speak out for Jesus in the world.

Paul Didn't Argue With God. When the Spirit of the Lord spoke to his heart, he began to pack his suitcase. On one occasion, he was leaving for Bithynia, but the Spirit suffered him not and he didn't go. Then he saw the vision of the Macedonian man and right away he left for Macedonia. Obedience is the greatest attribute of the child of God.

Paul Was Not Afraid of a Goal. He knew where he was going. He pressed toward the mark of the prize of the high calling of God in Christ Jesus (see Phil. 3:14). He also knew what it was going to cost him to get there, yet he still refused to ease up. Thank God for a man who would not be lukewarm, halfhearted or casual with God's business! Christians have no business living on "HALFWAY BOULEVARD."

For those who agree and desire to move to a more active life of service for God, I suggest you get some new furniture moved into your new home at the corner of Busy Street and Active Avenue. Notice the seven things that ought to be a part of your life.

I. The Go of Commission

God told Abraham to go, and he went. So did Moses, Joshua, Elijah, Peter, Paul, the Blind Man, the Adulterous Woman, the Maniac of Gadara and many others. He gave us the Great Commission as a last, dying request.

Isaiah got a glimpse of the Lord one day and became troubled about his sinful condition. Just as soon as that was taken care of, he wanted to go. He volunteered himself and cried out, "Here am I; send me" (Isa. 6:8). It is normal for a person to want to go with God's message. There is something wrong when we do not want to go.

II. The Glow of Compassion

Compassion will develop and grow as we are exposed to the need. The psalmist explains this: "He that goeth forth and weepeth; bearing precious seed, shall doubtless come again with rejoicing, bringing his sheaves with him" (Ps. 126:6). Jesus had compassion on the multitudes and wept over the city of Jerusalem. Paul ceased not to warn the people with tears day and night.

I remember one night visiting in a home where I was trying to win the husband to Christ. He was polite but hard. "No, I'll not do that," he said several times. Then I noticed his little wife began to weep silently. When he saw the tears running down her cheeks, he fell down on his knees. Compassion had brought results again.

III. The Grip of Conviction

When a person makes a commitment to God, it ought to grip his soul. His mind ought to be made up at that point that the Bible is right and that settles it! There used to be a day when right was right and wrong was wrong, but that day is gone. Gray has replaced black and white and we are in a mess.

In the Bible, men knew where they stood. Paul said, "For I know whom I have believed, and am persuaded that he is able to keep that which I have committed unto him against that day" (II Tim. 1:12). When specific convictions grip a man, they will give him purpose and direction.

IV. The Godliness of Consecration

People are moving farther and farther out of town in this matter. David prophesied that "the godly man ceaseth from among the children of men" (Ps. 12:1). Paul pleaded with men to "present your bodies a living sacrifice, holy, acceptable unto God, which is your reasonable service" (Rom. 12:1). The Bible says of Caleb, "He hath wholly followed the Lord" (Deut. 1:36). O God, may his tribe increase!

I was recently conducting a revival service in Grace Baptist Church of Wilmington, North Carolina. It was on Mother's Day.

A sweet little lady was presented with a corsage for being the oldest mother present. She was seventy-nine. She had been in all the meetings that week. During the invitation, a very attractive well-to-do, middle-aged lady came forward weeping and was saved. She was asked to give her testimony. "Thank God for my godly mother here this morning. I have watched her for years and I want to thank her for showing me Christ."

This was the daughter of the seventy-nine-year-old lady. There was much weeping and rejoicing by the whole congregation. Godly living had paid off again.

V. The Grace of Consistency

Don't you get tired of once-in-a-whilers, used-to-be'ers and later-on'ers? The churches today are full of spasmodic, part-time Christians who are an abomination to God. They have just enough religion to make them miserable.

This crowd gets real stirred up during revival meetings, then they are gone again. The Word of God declares, "Be ye stedfast, unmoveable, always abounding in the work of the Lord, forasmuch as ye know your labour is not in vain in the Lord" (I Cor. 15:58). Thank God for Moses who refused to be scared off by the Pharaoh, Daniel who would not stop praying, the Hebrew children who would not bow down, Joseph who would not have any part of Potiphar's wife, and for Jesus who told the Devil, "It is written. . ." (see Matt. 4:4,7,10).

In season or out of season, God give us grace to stand.

VI. The Gumption of Compatibility

This fifty-dollar word has a one-thousand-dollar meaning. It simply means to have common sense in any situation. God works through common sense. The Holy Spirit gives us spiritual discernment. He gives us sense enough to say and to do the right thing at the right time.

Philip didn't know exactly what he was going to say to the eunuch. He joined himself to the chariot and started talking. It wasn't long before he led the eunuch to Christ and he baptized him. Jesus talked to farmers about sowing and reaping, fishermen about fishing, shepherds about sheep, and carpenters about a building with a good foundation. That is gumption!

VII. The Grit of Continuance

People who are determined to please God must learn the lesson of persistence. Moses endured, as seeing Him who is invisible. James said, "Blessed is the man who endureth temptation: for when he is tried, he shall receive the crown of life. . ." (James 1:12).

Jacob would not let go of the angel until he got the blessing. Moses would not quit fasting and praying until God changed His mind and spared the people. Elisha refused to let Elijah get out of his sight until the mantle was his. The Gentile woman refused to get offended until she got the crumbs from the table. Blind Bartimaeus just hollered louder when they tried to keep him quiet, so serious was he about getting his sight back. All of these accounts show us the value of staying with it until the desired result comes.

Torrey Johnson tells how he was traveling recently on a plane. He was praying that the Lord would give him an opportunity to witness to someone. The air became turbulent and the stewardess sat down next to him until it calmed. He engaged her in conversation and won her to Christ. As he departed from the plane in St. Louis, she said, "If I don't see you again, I'll see you in Heaven."

A few minutes later a radio announcement told of the crash of that very same plane. The girl was killed with the rest of the passengers and crew. What a blessing that Mr. Johnson did not just halfway do his job!

God help us to get into God's business with our whole heart and get off "HALFWAY BOULEVARD."

The World's Most Popular Religion

"*. . .after the straitest sect of our religion I lived a Pharisee.*"—Acts 26:5.

At this time of the year, religion is a very popular subject. Palm Sunday and Easter Sunday will draw great throngs of people out to church.

Before his salvation experience on the road to Damascus, the Apostle Paul was one of the most religious men of his time. In Acts 26:5 he states, ". . .after the most straitest sect of our religion I lived a Pharisee." All of us know, of course, that he was not a Christian. In fact, he was anti-Christian and anti-Christ, committing to prison and even murdering those who followed after the Lord Jesus. His testimony, as recorded through the Scriptures, tells us that he was very, very religious.

Of course, the world is plagued with religion. Religion is a bigger tool to prevent people from going to Heaven than it is for getting them there. Man is basically a religious creature. He is going to worship something or somebody. The Hindu has his Shasta. He worships cows, rivers and creatures. The Persian has his Zend-Avesta. The Hebrew has his Talmud. The Chinese has his Confucius or his Mao Tse-Tung. The Japanese has his Shinto shrine or Buddha god-shelf. The Roman had his Sybiline. The Mohammedan has his Koran. And the Moslem bows toward Mecca. In these last months we've seen the rise of the Moonies, the Har Krishnas, Herbert W. Armstrong with his World

Tomorrow and Radio Church of God. The Mormons are everywhere. Jehovah's Witnesses always beat the Baptists to the mission fields of the world. The Seventh-Day Adventists, the Christian Scientists and all the others mingle like leaven through bread in our society.

Religion is broken down into hundreds of different denominations. There are Jews, Catholic, Greek Orthodox, Lutheran, Episcopalian, Presbyterian, Church of God, Church of Christ, Nazarene, Unity, Apostolic, Reform, Anglican, the Gay Church, Church of Satan, and dozens of different kinds of Baptists. There are the American Baptists, German Baptists, Swedish Baptists, Southern Baptists, Conservative Baptists, General Baptists, General Association of Regular Baptists, Old Regular Baptists, Hard-shell Baptists, Primitive Baptists, Missionary Baptists, Independent Baptists and even Lily Baptists. As Vance Havner says, "The Lily Baptists are called that because, in the words of Jesus, 'They do not toil; neither do they spin.' "

Now, which is the right religion? Religion is mentioned only five times in the Bible: (1) in our text, (2 and 3) in Galatians 1:13,14 and (4 and 5) in James 1:26,27. In reality, it's found only in three places, but the word itself is used five times.

Ezekiel said, ". . .for with their mouth they shew much love, but their heart goeth after covetousness. . .they hear thy words, but they do not do them" (33:31,32). Paul tells us in Titus 1:16, "They profess that they know God, but in words they deny him." Again in II Timothy 3:5 he says, "Having a form of godliness, but denying the power thereof." Jesus told of those who "love to pray standing in the synagogues and in the corner of the streets, that they may be seen of men" (Matt. 6:5).

The world seems to want a religion that will accept them as they are, without challenge; a religion that goes along with what they already believe; a religion that will not object to what they now do; or a religion that will let all men be brothers and still believe whatever they want to believe. Popular religion today is one that does not insist, does not involve, does not interfere and does not include.

I. Religion That Does Not Insist

A religion that will be popular and cause folk to rally around it will be one that does not insist on. . .

1. *Repentance.* Remember, Jesus said, "Except ye repent, ye shall all likewise perish."

2. *Regeneration.* This will not be included in the popular religion, but the Bible insists that, "Ye must be born again."

3. *Restitution.* The popular religion will not insist on making right the wrongs or straightening out those things you've done that can be made right again.

4. *Retribution.* It will not insist on retribution and eternal Hell at the end of a sinful life.

A lot of people will come as long as there is not "insist" in your religion.

II. Religion That Does Not Involve

The popular religion does not include. . .

1. *Book Without Error.* Our Bible is the infallible, inspired, inerrant Word of God. Many people would like to have it be just a manual of religion.

2. *Blessed Hope.* The Bible teaches the second coming of the Lord Jesus Christ. It is involved in God's type of religion, but not man's.

3. *Blood Atonement.* The lamb died in Eden; Cain's offering was rejected, while Abel's was accepted. Abraham offered Isaac and God substituted the lamb. "The life of the flesh is in the blood" (Lev. 17:11). ". . .ye were not redeemed with corruptible things, as silver and gold. . .but with the precious blood of Christ" (I Pet. 1:18,19). The Bible teaches that redemption involves blood atonement.

III. Religion That Does Not Interfere

Popular religion does not interfere with pleasures, customs, habits, jobs, families and plans. If you can come up with a religion that will let man be, do, and go when and where he wants to, without having any interference, it will be popular. In other words, most people want a religious coat that they can put on when they go to church, take off and hang on the closet door when they get home, and never bring it out again until the next Sunday, or maybe next Easter or Christmas.

IV. Religion That Does Not Include

Religion will be popular if it does not include *obligation and responsibility.* David said, "Shall I make sacrifice of that which doth cost me nothing?" There is responsibility in true Christianity, but great religious systems are so glad to have people join with them that they are perfectly willing to put up with anybody and anything.

We are responsible for. . .

1. *Cleanliness.* Bible Christianity includes a clean heart, clean mind and clean hands.

2. *Concern.* God expects us to have burden and interest in others.

3. *Conduct.* Our behavior is based on what we believe.

In closing, let me point out that the person who accepts these basic steps of responsibility will find the truth of the book of Hebrews: "The commandments of the Lord are not grievous." Christians rejoice in being able to serve, sacrifice and surrender their rights to those of God as taught in the Bible. The most popular religions of the world are just that—religions of the world, not religions of the Bible or of God.

There is a great need today to preach the true Gospel, the good news that Jesus Christ died on the cross and shed His blood to provide a plan of redemption to save our poor, lost souls.

Turn to Him today, if you don't already know Him as your Saviour. Then, write and tell us about it.

Born Again

"Marvel not that I said unto thee, Ye must be born again."—
John 3:7.

"Born again" has become a very popular term in these days.
Charles Colson of Watergate fame has been presented in a book
entitled *Born Again.* Jimmy Carter, all along his political trail,
talked about being a "born again" Christian. It hasn't shown up
much in the White House, however. Even Larry Flynt, the in-
famous pornographic editor of *The Hustler* Magazine, has been
using the term, because of his association with Ruth Carter
Stapleton, the President's sister. In spite of all this loose use of
the term, it's still a glowing and wonderful Bible term. It carries
with it a holy, sacred meaning, as well as feeling.

God seems to be an advocate of the "See it big, keep it simple"
philosophy. Someone added that the way to really make things
happen was to "See it big, keep it simple, and make it burn."
This Bible term, "born again," seems to have it all.

One dear old colored brother gave testimony to his experience
when he said, "I goes to church, I gives my money, I does the best
I can; then somebody comes along and says, 'Ye must be born
again.' "

John Wesley preached 3,782 times on "Why Ye Must Be Born
Again." Someone asked him, "Mr. Wesley, why do you preach so
much on 'Ye Must Be Born Again'?" His answer, "Because Ye
Must Be Born Again." Paul spoke one time about his natural
birth and nine times of the new birth.

Years ago someone illustrated that if a dead rabbit fell in the well, you could paint the pump, but that wouldn't improve the taste of the water. You might even build a new concrete foundation. That wouldn't do it either. You could put a new pump on the new foundation, but that still wouldn't do it. The only answer is to get that dead rabbit out of the well!

You can get a sinner new clothes, a new job and move him into a new house; you can teach him new language and habits; but until the old nature is replaced by a new nature by a spiritual-birth experience, he's still going to have that bad taste down inside. We do not need exterior decoration; we need interior regeneration. That's probably why Ghandi said, "If it weren't for Christians, I'd be one."

The new birth is not something you can explain. The new birth is something you must experience. It is a mystery that cannot be explained. It is a reality that cannot be explained away.

In his little book, *Flying Worms,* Dr. M. R. DeHaan explained the process of metamorphosis. The caterpillar gets into the cocoon and is transformed into a beautiful butterfly. No one can explain quite what happens. So it is with the new birth. Only God can explain that.

There are four things about the new birth that are important to us today.

I. It Is Individual

By this we mean *it is not by parents.* Covenant theology, a well-known religious philosophy, teaches that children born to two Christian parents automatically are under the covenant promise of God and are assured of salvation. However, the Bible says to these children the same as to the children born into the home of sinners, "Ye must be born again."

It is not by priests. It is not by proxy or by substitute or representative. No one can be born into God's family for you. The old-timers used to sing,

> You've got to walk that lonesome valley,
> You've got to go there by yourself.

**There's nobody here to go for you,
You've got to go there by yourself.**

They were referring to death, of course, but that same principle also applies to the new birth. Ye must be born again.

It is not by perception. In the testimony of Eldridge Cleaver, he claims he saw the face of Jesus and several religious personalities of the past in the moon in a vision. He claims he knew that he'd been born again because of this vision. It just doesn't work that way. There must be individual repentance and faith and individual acceptance of God's plan. It is individual.

II. It Is Instantaneous

Being born again is something like turning on a light. It happens right there on the spot. Dr. Fred Brown used to talk about turning off the light and trying to get in bed and get covered up before it went out. That would be pretty quick! The new birth is faster than that. When the Apostle Paul was brought in contact with the light of the Lord on the Damascus Road and heard the voice of the Lord, he cried out, "Who art thou, Lord?" If he knew it was the Lord, why did he cry out, "Who art thou, Lord?" If he knew who it was, why did he call him Lord? Surely, no one ought to call a person Lord unless they know who it is. The real truth is, Paul got saved between the words "thou" and "Lord."

Someone might say that you can't really get saved that quick. I heard about a man fixing some shingles on his roof. He caught his foot in the gutter spout and fell. A friend ran up to him and said, "Are you all right, Joe?"

When Joe answered in the affirmative, the man said, "Thank the Lord you're all right, Joe. You're not saved."

"Oh, yes I am," said Joe.

"Well, you weren't saved before," said the first man.

Joe answered, "I wasn't saved when I left the roof but I was when I hit the ground!"

A person can get saved mighty quick! The new birth is instantaneous.

III. It Is Indispensable

Ye *must* be born again. There is no other way to get around the salvation experience if a person intends to go to Heaven. Nicodemus was a very religious man, but he still had to be born again. He was a righteous man, but he still had to be born again. He was a rich man, yet he still had to be born again. He was a ruler; he still had to be born again. He was recognized, but he still needed to be born again.

Now, if a religious, righteous, rich ruler who was recognized by all the people needed to be born again, so do you and I.

The Old Testament prophet asked the question, "Can the Ethiopian change his skin? Can the leopard change his spots?" The answer is obviously no. The new birth is indispensable.

IV. It Is Initial

The new birth is the start of a brand new life. It is the beginning of our relationship to God. It is the doorway into Heaven. It is the earnest of the Spirit or the down payment of our salvation.

Years ago I visited a nuclear plant near Detroit. A man showed me all the flashing lights and clicking instruments in the large computer room. He explained the process of nuclear fission. Then he pointed to a little red button. He said, "When I pull up that little red button, everything in here comes alive. When I push it down, it all stops." It was the safety button to prevent accidents from happening in the nuclear plant.

He smiled and said to me, "That little red button represents faith. When faith is put into action, it opens up everything— God, Heaven and all of the good things that God has prepared for us and has given to us. If faith is dead and the button is pushed down, then we are in the dark and nothing is alive."

The new birth is like that little red button; it is the beginning, and it gets everything started.

I trust you, my dear friend, have been born again. If not, I want to encourage you to get this matter settled as soon as possible.

In our living room at home we have an old antique clock that used to run for several days, after being wound. When we moved to Louisville and put it on the mantle, we could never get it started again. It sat there on the fireplace mantle for seven years. Praying right near that clock one morning at the beginning of the year, I suddenly became aware of the fact that it was running.

The old clock had been dusted every week, but sat there to look at. On this particular Friday, when it was dusted, the jar or movement sat the thing in motion and it started to run. It must have been running for a couple of days when I became aware of it. I thought, "That old dead clock has been lifeless and useless for seven years; now, suddenly, it has come to life."

So it is with many a sinner that comes into contact with Christ. The brush with the Lord brings them into action. They begin to be useful again.

Jabez

"And Jabez was more honourable than his brethren: and his mother called his name Jabez, saying, Because I bare him with sorrow. And Jabez called on the God of Israel, saying, Oh that thou wouldest bless me indeed, and enlarge my coast, and that thine hand might be with me, and that thou wouldest keep me from evil, that it may not grieve me! And God granted him that which he requested."—I Chron. 4:9,10.

I've asked more than one hundred congregations how many have ever heard of Jabez. Usually just one or two people in the whole congregation, if any, will raise their hands. This was always quite a puzzle to me, because he is such a favorite character of mine.

This brings up a good question. Why doesn't anybody know Jabez? I think I found the answer. I believe that many times in a church the pastor will suggest that the congregation read the Bible through in a year's time by reading three chapters every weekday and five chapters on Sunday. This can be accomplished by December 31. On that date, you will be finishing Revelation 22:20.

When we begin, we read the tremendous story of the Creation, the creation of man, Adam and Eve in the Garden of Eden, the awful story of sin entering in through the serpent that beguiled Eve. We read the exciting story of Noah and deliverance from the Flood by the ark, the tower of Babel experience, the call of Abraham, the stories of Isaac, Jacob, Esau and Joseph. All of this is very exciting reading. Most people will not stop at reading three chapters a day, but will get far ahead during these early days of the year.

Then we get into the book of Exodus and find the children of Israel down in Egypt. We see Moses being called at the Burning Bush to go bring God's people home. Then comes the exciting account of the passover, the story of Moses delivering the children of Israel across the Red Sea into the Wilderness journeys. We read of all the marvelous accounts of God's provisions of manna, clothing that would not wear out, water out of the rock, the brass serpent on a pole, the Tabernacle and all the rest. Finally, we get into the book of Leviticus where things slow down a bit, because of all the laws and feasts and offerings of the Jews.

Through the book of Numbers and into Deuteronomy things speed back up again. We watch with excitement the conquest of Canaan and read about the exciting life of Samson, Jephthah and the rest of the Judges. Then comes the beautiful love story of Ruth and Boaz; into I and II Samuel where we are thrilled with the stories of Saul, David and Solomon. In the books of I and II Kings, we read of God's great prophets, Elijah and Elisha.

Then we come to I Chronicles. In the first chapter we read, "Adam, Sheth, Enosh, Kenan, Mahalaleel, Jered, Henoch, Methuselah, Lamech, Noah, Shem, Ham and Japheth" (1-4). As you analyze chapter 1 of I Chronciles, you will find that it is names, names and more names. In fact, almost 250 names are in this chapter alone. In chapter 2 you will find, "These are the sons of Israel; Reuben, Simeon, Levi and Judah, Issachar and Zebulun, Dan, Joseph and Benjamin, Naphtali, Gad, and Asher" (1,2). Names, names and more names again!

In chapter 3 of I Chronicles we read, "Now these were the sons of David, which were born unto him in Hebron. . .," and we have still more names. When we get to the 4th chapter we start through a long series of names again: "The sons of Judah; Pharez, Hezron and Carmi, and Hur, and Shobal" (1).

I am convinced that people begin to skip over because all of these names are hard and do not mean anything personally. I believe that most people miss the 9th and 10th verses of chapter

4 because they take for granted that all of these names will mean nothing.

But now, you need to wait just a minute and consider verse 9. That is where Jabez is found.

Why did God bury Jabez down under all of these hundreds of other names? Did He not want us to know about this man? I believe God hid him away from us because of the particular message he had. God seems to save him until some particular time when we will need him.

First of all, Jabez was more honorable than his brethren. To be honorable is a tremendous attribute, but it does not mean that he is saved. We cannot be satisfied just because he was honorable. There are a lot of folks in your town and mine who pay all their bills, love their wives and children, work hard on the job, but will die and go to Hell, simply because they have not been born again. To be honorable is just not enough. The Bible says, "For man looketh on the outward appearance, but the Lord looketh on the heart" (I Sam. 16:7).

Then consider, too, that Jabez' name means "sorrow," "burden" or "miserable." Can you imagine what a hard time this little fellow must have had when he was a boy? His name meant misery. Maybe some of the children came knocking on the door, asking if Misery could come out and play. What a name! The Bible says that his mother called him Jabez because she had borne him in sorrow (I Chron. 4:9). A hard time at birth had labeled his name.

All Bible names have meanings. But in the Bible every name has a specific and definite meaning given of God with a spiritual message behind it. Jabez' name means "burden" and "sorrow." I want you to notice he was made into an honorable man because of his problems and burdens. People who have been through a lot of burdens and problems will be refined and cultured into honorable persons.

Notice that Jabez called on the God of Israel. He is starting to pray. Now, we are getting somewhere spiritually. Even though he is honorable and has been through a whole lot of trouble, that doesn't mean that he is going to Heaven. Now, at least, he is calling on God. I want us to listen quietly to what Jabez is asking.

I. Grace

Jabez called on the God of Israel and asked for the blessing of God (I Chron. 4:10). Of course, the blessing of God begins with the grace of God. The Bible explains to us in Ephesians 2:8,9: "For by grace are ye saved through faith; and that not of yourselves: it is the gift of God: Not of works, lest any man should boast." In Hebrews 4:16 we are encouraged, "Let us therefore come boldly unto the throne of grace, that we may obtain mercy, and find grace to help in time of need." If a person is going to come to God, he has to start at the starting place and receive the gift of God and the grace of God.

I remember a man who came to see me some years ago at the request of his wife. This man was a very important man. He was a man of position and power, but he was an alcoholic. He wanted to quit. He asked me for advice and counsel. I opened the Bible and started to read Romans, chapter 3, but he stopped me saying, "There is no need to read that. I don't believe anything that fellow Paul had to say."

I said, "Well, I am sorry, Sir. I'll read John, chapter 3."

Again he stopped me. He didn't believe anything that John said either. "In fact," he said, "I don't believe anything in the New Testament."

Then I turned quickly to Isaiah, chapter 53. I thought of how Philip explained to the eunuch how to be saved from this portion. Maybe I could help him to understand the simple Gospel.

"It is no use, Preacher," he said. "I don't care anything about what Isaiah had to say either."

"Do you believe any of the Bible?" I asked him.

A little tear came out of his eye and started down his cheek and he said, "I dearly love Psalm 23. Would you read that?"

I turned to it and began to read. "The Lord is my shepherd." He is not, I told him. "I shall not want." You will too. "He maketh me to lie down in green pastures." He does not. "He leadeth me beside the still waters." No, He doesn't. "He restoreth my soul." He does not.

I read it, phrase by phrase, robbing him of every portion. I explained to him that if he would not take Romans 3, John 3 and Isaiah 53, then he couldn't have Psalm 23. The man sobbed. I asked him to get on his knees with me for prayer, and he did. He cried some more. But when I asked him to repent and accept Christ, he would not do it. He stood, thanked me for my time, and left the house.

The thing he wanted was for me to pray that God might deliver him from his alcohol and wrecked physical body, but when I suggested that he needed the Lord Jesus Christ and the grace of God, he disagreed and would not accept it. He did not start in the starting place. Thank God, Jabez realized that he must start with grace!

II. Growth

Jabez prayed, "Oh that thou wouldest bless me indeed and enlarge my coast" (II Chron. 4:10). He was not satisfied to remain the same. He was interested in growing in grace. In I Peter 2:2 we read, ". . .desire the sincere milk of the word, that ye may grow thereby." In II Peter 3:18 we see, "But grow in grace and in the knowledge of our Lord and Saviour Jesus Christ." It is important that a Christian grow, and Jabez was praying for that growth.

I made a visit on a back street in Elkton, Maryland, one day and found a lady who had a very humble little home. I read the Bible and prayed with her. I was about to leave when I heard a little gurgling sound out of the next room. She said, "Excuse me while I take care of the bably."

I didn't know these folks had a baby and said so.

"Oh," she said, "let me show him to you."

I went through the doorway into the next room and there I saw the most pitiful little body I had ever seen. The little boy had large knees and ankles, big elbows and a large head with hair. He had teeth. He looked like he was about four years old, but he had on a diaper and was sucking a baby bottle. When I asked her how old he was, the mother told me he was eighteen. I asked her what was wrong with him. She said, "The doctor said that he just never grew right."

I felt terrible. When I left the house I went straight to the church and spent the next couple of hours locked in my office. I didn't want to see anybody. Then I began to think about the people in our congregation, how many that had never grown. I began to think of the need of preaching on this subject to our people.

The next Sunday I preached on "Spiritual Deformity"—not growing in grace—and God moved our hearts.

Jabez wanted to grow.

III. Guidance

Jabez prayed for the hand of the Lord to be upon him. He wanted the guidance and leadership of the Lord. In Matthew 4:1 and Luke 4, we read of Jesus being led by the Spirit into the wilderness. In Romans 8:14 we read again, "For as many as are led by the Spirit of God, they are the sons of God." We read when the children of Israel in the Old Testament were led through the wilderness by a cloud and a pillar of fire.

Dr. Lee Roberson came to our church one time to talk to our teachers and officers. A little boy sitting on the front row was very interested. Dr. Roberson asked the boy to come to the platform. He did so. Dr. Roberson took hold of his hand and began to talk to all of us. The little boy was so embarrassed that he forgot all about what Dr. Roberson was saying and began to respond to the tug of his hand.

Dr. Roberson walked sideways, backward and forward across the platform; the little fellow was completely under his control. Then he said, "If you really want to be used of God, learn this simple lesson. Let God be in complete control to lead you and guide you in His will."

Of course, we all got the lesson.

Jabez prayed for the guidance of the Lord.

IV. Godliness

Jabez prayed that God would deliver him from evil or keep

him away from sin. This means godliness. Psalm 12:1 prophesies that the godly men will cease from the earth. This prophecy seems to have been completed. First Timothy 4:7 admonishes us ". . .exercise thyself rather unto godliness." Titus 2:12 says "we should live soberly, righteously, and godly, in this present world." Second Peter 1:6 encourages us to add "to knowledge temperance; and to temperance patience; and to patience godliness."

I remember a long time ago a little white-haired lady coming to our church and sitting on the second row. I preached for several Sundays and hoped that she would join our church by letter.

One day she did come forward, not to join by letter, but to be saved! I was amazed that she wasn't already a Christian. She was baptized and began to walk for God. This eighty-three-old lady never missed a service. She came rain or shine. She was there for prayer meeting as well as for all other services.

We had a tent meeting for five weeks, and she never missed a night. When I went out to visit, folks would complain of being tired and worn out, of not being able to get to the services because of heavy schedules. But I always reminded them that Mrs. Roark would be there.

Then this sweet, godly woman got sick and finally she died. For two solid years she walked for God day and night. Everyone loved her. As I stood by her casket in the funeral home, the people began to come and one after another made such statements as, "My, what a godly soul!" "She was a godly person, wasn't she?" On and on they praised her life. My heart was greatly blessed to hear the people attribute to this woman the characteristics of godliness. It made me want to live a more godly, righteous life.

Jabez seemed to be praying for that in his life. He prayed for GRACE, GROWTH, GUIDANCE and for GODLINESS. Our text says,

"And God granted him that which he requested."—I Chron. 4:10.

Unfinished Business

"When Jesus therefore had received the vinegar, he said, IT IS FINISHED: and he bowed his head, and gave up the ghost."— John 19:30.

God has certainly left none of His work unfinished. In creation He worked diligently for six days; then the heavens and the earth were finished (Gen. 2:1). God rested then, but only after He had completed the work.

Moses learned this valuable lesson from God. God had commissioned him to oversee the building of the huge and elaborate Tabernacle in the Wilderness. Thousands of details were to be carried out. Certain metals were to be used, and particular colors were important. In a multitude of ways, the Tabernacle was to be a type of Christ. We read in Exodus 39:32, "Thus was all the work of the tabernacle of the tent of the congregation finished: and the children of Israel did according to all that the Lord commanded Moses, so did they." Aren't you glad they did not call a strike and stop short of completing this building?

When Nehemiah built the wall, he faced unsurmountable problems. He fought discouragement, fear, doubt and much opposition. There were plenty of reasons why it couldn't be done, but he did it just the same! We read these words of victory, "So the wall was finished in the twenty and fifth day of the month Elul, in fifty and two days" (Neh. 6:15)

According to the laws of aviation, the bumblebee can't fly, but no one has ever bothered to tell him, so he flies over 800 miles per hour. Someone has said, "The man who says it can't be done usually gets run over by the fellows who are doing it."

Lying on his deathbed, Paul the apostle gave a testimony that ought to strengthen our get-up-and-go. He said, "I have finished my course. . ." (II Tim. 4:7). Jesus gathered His disciples around Him just before His death and prayed His great intercessory prayer. "I have finished the work which thou gavest me to do" (John 17:4). Now, just a few days later, He is crying out from the cross, *"Tetelestai,"* meaning complete. It is translated, "It is finished" (John 19:30).

Let us notice some things that were not left unfinished.

I. Complete Redemption

Jesus paid it all,
  All to Him I owe.
Sin had left a crimson stain,
  He washed it white as snow.

No one can accuse Jesus of unfinished business. He did not renege or fall short of His responsibility.

One man boarded a city bus with what he thought was a transfer ticket. He handed it to the driver, who sharply called out, "Oh, He did, did He?"

By mistake the man had given him a tract entitled, "Jesus Paid It All." Now, Jesus didn't pay your bus fare, but He did completely pay your way to Heaven.

Peter emphasizes that, ". . .ye were not redeemed with corruptible things, as silver and gold, from your vain conversation received by tradition from your fathers; But with the precious blood of Christ. . ." (I Pet. 1:18,19).

Paul elaborates, ". . .know ye not that. . .ye are not your own? For ye are bought with a price: therefore glorify God in your body, and in your spirit, which are God's" (I Cor. 6:19).

II. Complete Regeneration

When Jesus Christ saves us, we are saved all the way. We are given everlasting life and that lasts for all eternity. It is eternal. When He comes into our hearts, we have all of Him.

We are not saved in stages. We do not need a second work of grace before we can get in. Our Bible does not say ye must be born again, and again, and again.

Some years ago, a lady told me, "I used to be saved." She commented, "I lived right for two years."

"Are you sure you had eternal life?" I asked.

"Oh, I'm positive," she added.

"Why didn't it last for eternity?" I reasoned.

I suggested that she had two years' life and that wasn't the kind God promised. He promised everlasting life.

God doesn't do things halfway. He makes all things new. He completely regenerates.

III. Complete Revelation

The Bible was not complete in New Testament days. Paul explained, "For we know in part, and we prophesy in part. But when that which is perfect is come, then that which is in part shall be done away" (I Cor. 13:9,10). He was referring to the completion of the Bible as we know it.

In the Old Testament, men were instructed by visions and the voice of God speaking from a bush, a cloud or an angel. On one occasion, we are told that "there was no open vision" (I Sam. 3:1). Every man did that which was right in his own eyes.

After the book of Daniel was written, he was instructed, "O Daniel, shut up the words, and seal the book, even to the time of the end" (12:4). In contrast to this, the book of Revelation, a parallel to Daniel, was not to be sealed, "for the time is at hand" (22:10).

A solemn word of warning was then given about adding anything to the prophecy of this book. In other words, the Bible is a complete revelation. It tells us all we need to know about God and His plan for us.

IV. Complete Rapture

There are many views concerning the return of Christ to the earth. Some hold to a postmillennial view, others to an amillennial view, and still others a premillennial view.

Among the premillennial crowd, there are pretribulation, midtribulation and posttribulation views. Now, there has come forth a group advocating a partial rapture. These folks believe that only a certain, dedicated group of believers will be taken in the rapture.

There are two distinct groups of people living today—the lost and the saved. All the living saved will be "caught up" at the coming of Christ (I Thess. 4:17). Also the saved dead will be raised and caught up together with the living (I Thess. 4:13-18). No lost people, living or dead, will be involved.

The rapture will include every born-again, blood-bought child of God. It will be a complete rapture.

V. Complete Repentance

Here is where the trouble comes in. This is the unfinished business. God has done His part. He has completed redemption, regeneration, revelation and will completely rapture us, but we have not completely repented.

Repentance means unconditional surrender. It suggests wholly submitting to another's will. There is a vast difference, too, between penance and repentance. Judas did penance by giving back the silver. Peter repented and wept bitterly.

Jesus said, ". . .except ye repent, ye shall all likewise perish" (Luke 13:3).

Peter said, "Repent, and be baptized every one of you in the name of Jesus Christ for the remission of sins. . ." (Acts 2:38).

Paul said, "And the times of this ignorance God winked at; but now commandeth all men every where to repent" (Acts 17:30).

John wrote, ". . .repent, and do the first works; or else I will come unto thee quickly, and will remove thy candlestick out of his place, except thou repent" (Rev. 2:5).

To the sinner, without repentance there is no salvation. To the child of God, without complete, wholehearted, full repentance, there will be no power to overcome, no peace that passes all understanding, no joy unspeakable, no cup running over and no abundant life.

God did His part; let us do ours. Repent, submit, yield, dedicate, give in, surrender, turn, sanctify ourselves and commit completely to Him—now!

Dividing Mankind—
The Jew, the Gentile
and the Church

There are many different ways of dividing men. We might divide them politically into communists, capitalists or Christians. We might divide them as to race. They would fall into the categories of Asian, Negroid, or Anglo-Saxon. Denominationally, they might be divided into Baptists, Methodists, Presbyterians, Catholics, etc.—maybe more than 700 different preferences. We could also divide men into two distinct groups: saved men on their way to Heaven, and lost men on their way to Hell. However, the Bible clearly divided men into three groups: "The Jew, the Gentile and the church."

Paul speaks to us in I Corinthians 10:32 saying, "Give none offense to the Jew, nor to the Gentiles, nor to the church of God." In this message, I would like to deal with those three divisions. First of all. . .

I. The "Jew"

Jews fall into four categories. There is first, the extreme orthodox. Most of these are in Palestine today. Second, there is the orthodox; third, conservative and fourth, reform.

Someone has said the word "JEW" stands for "Jehovah's Eternal Witness." The Jews have been around a long time. There are 6.1 million of them in the United States, 2.7 million of them in Israel and 2.6 million Jews in Russia. However, their religious influence seems to be declining. Synagogues are closing in the

United States at the rate of twenty-five per year. Out of 4 billion in the world, only 14 million are Jewish (one-third of one percent of the population). It is interesting to note that in the last few years twelve percent of the Nobel Prize winners in physics, chemistry and medicine have been Jews. Karl Marx, the father of communism, was a Jew; but, so was Jesus Christ, the Father of Christianity.

When Disraeli, the English statesman, was taunted by an English lord because of his Jewish birth, he replied, "Sir, my ancestors were princes and kings in the earth when yours were raving savages."

The Jews have the purest blood on earth today. For almost five thousand years, they've maintained their identity. Their average lifespan is one-third longer than ours. They have eaten and lived according to the laws given to Moses by God. Frederick the Great asked a court preacher for the unanswerable proof of the inspiration of the Bible. He answered, "The Jew, my master, the Jew."

In a day of spreading anti-Semitism, no Christian will hate the Jew. He taught you of your God, your Christ and gave you your Bible.

The Bible makes a distinction between a Hebrew, an Israelite and a Jew. A Hebrew is a descendant of Abraham; an Israelite denotes of Jacob and a Jew denotes of Judah.

The Jew has been around a long time. Water failed to drown him—consider Moses. Gallows failed to hang him—consider Mordecai. Fires failed to burn him—consider the Hebrews in the fiery furnace. Lions failed to eat him—consider Daniel. Persecution has failed to destroy him—consider the Israelis and their Six-Day War.

It all started in Genesis 12:1. Adam was not a Jew. Noah was not a Jew. Abraham was a Jew. God called him out of Ur of the Chaldees and promised to make his seed as the sand of the sea, the stars of the sky and the dust of the earth (see Gen. 12:2,3; 13:16). Abraham gave birth to Isaac after the experience with Hagar and Ishmael. At Mount Moriah, it appeared that God had changed His mind and would do away with Isaac, the promised seed; but, the deliverance of Isaac through a miraculous experience made way for Jacob and Esau to be born. From Jacob came the twelve tribes of Israel: Reuben, Simeon, Levi, Zebulun, Judah, Issachar, Gad, Dan, Naphtali, Asher, Benjamin and Joseph.

After the twelve tribes were being assigned their ground into the land of Palestine, it was not long until they were under the reign and rule of judges. People tired of the judges soon and wanted to do that which was right in their own eyes. They began to cry out for a king. God gave them Saul and then David, then Solomon.

The prophets also were very prominent on the scene, giving the prediction of that which would come to pass in the history of Israel and giving us a preview of things to come in the future. Jesus Christ, the Son of God, born of a virgin of the tribe of Judah, from the house of David, soon was involved in the story of the Jew.

I suppose the saddest words in all the Bible can be found in John 1:11: "He came unto his own, and his own received him not." Because of the rejection of Jesus as Messiah, they are put completely out of the picture. Romans, chapters 9, 10 and 11 tell us that Israel has been blinded in part. Individually, some Jews are being saved, but the nation of Israel has rejected the Messiah and, as a whole, they are in spiritual darkness.

During the tribulation period on the earth, the two witnesses who are resurrected from the dead, spoken of in Revelation, chapter 11, will win 144,000 Jewish evangelists. They will go forth and win the nation of Israel to Christ in a day. They will accept Him as their own personal Messiah. Following that, they will play a very definite and prominent part in the thousand-year reign upon the earth. God will turn back to the Jew during the tribulation and during the millennium.

II. The "Gentile"

The story of the Gentile begins in the Book of Daniel, chapter 2, with the vision of Nebuchadnezzar. Nebuchadnezzar was king of Babylon. Babylon was descended from the people who built the Tower of Babel, whose tongues were confused.

The image that Nebuchadnezzar saw and couldn't remember until Daniel came and revealed the meaning to him, was a huge, giant statue. The statue had a golden head, silver shoulders, brass mid-section, iron hips and iron and clay feet and toes. He watched, until a great stone, cut out of the mountain without hands, came down from Heaven, smashed against the image and broke it to pieces. Then it ground the image to powder and blew it away like chaff from the threshingfloor.

Daniel explained to the king that the golden head was the Babylonian Empire; that the silver represented the Medo-Persian Empire that would come on the scene after the first empire was dissolved. The brass represented the great Greek Empire under Alexander the Great; the iron represented the Roman Empire that would conquer the world and rule from the East to the West. Iron and clay feet and toes seemed to suggest a communistic, capitalistic conflict between the ten countries of the ten sections of the Roman Empire. Those ten divisions of the Roman Empire were absorbed into the history of the world, until recently when the nations of the European Common Market began to bring it all back into focus.

For about two thousand years now, there has been a discontinuation of the prophecy recorded in Daniel, chapter 2. This is the Period of Grace, or the Church Age that was revealed to Paul in Ephesians, chapter 3. The stone cut without hands was the beautiful experience of the coming of the Lord Jesus Christ in great power and glory to overcome the remaining kingdoms of the world and grind up the teachings of their culture, philosophies and spread them out to the corners of the earth, replacing them with the beautiful kingdom of God on earth for one thousand years of millennial reign.

III. The "Church"

In Acts, chapter 2, we read of those who were added to the church. Jesus, of course, began to gather people together and plant them into a family or into a kingdom. The Holy Spirit came on the day of Pentecost and launched the church into action. At Pentecost, three thousand Jews became a part of a local assembly. In Acts, chapter 10 a second Pentecost experience referred to as the Gentile Pentecost baptized a great host of people into that same union.

Local churches began to spring up everywhere the disciples went. As people received Christ as Saviour, they were baptized into the local church. In Romans 3:9 we read that there is no distinction between the Jew and the Gentile; "They are all under sin." In Romans 10:12-13 we read there is no difference, "for the same Lord over all is rich unto all that call upon him. For whosoever shall call upon the name of the Lord shall be saved." If a Jew or Gentile comes in his sin and flees from judgment to receive Christ as his personal Saviour and Messiah, he is born into a third group.

The Lord is working now during the church age, until the rapture, when He will redeem all of His children out of this world by resurrection or rapture and take them into the presence of the Heavenly Father for the judgment seat of Christ and the marriage feast. Then they will return to the earth for the millennial reign.

It is imperative that, whether a person be Jew or Gentile, he become a member of the family of God by receiving the Lord Jesus Christ as personal Saviour and Messiah.

Years ago I read of the tragedy of the dew. I had never thought of dew as being tragic. It is beautiful! It sparkles on the meadows at night when the moon is shining, and it looks like the diamonds over the meadow when the sun touches it early in the morning. Yet the article said that, as the process of evaporation was discontinued in the cool of the evening, some of the water that was being transferred to heaven by the rays of the sun was cut off because of the temperature change. That moisture fell back to earth. The author called it "water that started for heaven too late," and, of course, it missed out.

It is likely that some of the readers of this article may wait too late to get the matter settled in your heart about what is going to happen to you when you die. I trust you will not be like the dew.

Past the Moon

It is my duty to warn you who read these words that you may not get to finish this sermon before the Lord shall descend from the heavens in fulfillment of the Bible promise, "I will come again. . ." (John 14:3). In this day, when men are spending billions to reach the moon and more billions trying to find God's secret of how to re-enter the earth's atmosphere, the time is ripe for Jesus Christ to ignore the problems of space and return to earth to receive His own unto Himself (John 14:3). The born-again child of God will be caught up into the heavens past the moon, sun and all the planets, to a place prepared for him by the Son of God.

In Isaiah 14:13, we find the words very characteristic of this age. "I will ascend into heaven, I will exalt my throne above the stars of God." In Isaiah 14:14, we read, "I will ascend above the heights of the clouds." These words may sound like Russia in her race for space control or even the U.S. in her bid for top spot in the heavens, but actually they are the words of Lucifer (the Devil) when he decided to overthrow God's throne. God didn't allow this, but threw him out of Heaven down upon the earth and pronounced the judgment of the lake of fire for him (See Rev. 20:10).

Again, in Genesis 11:4, we find similar words, ". . .let us build us a city and a tower, whose top may reach unto heaven; and let us make us a name, lest we be scattered abroad upon the face of the whole earth." Men have always had a desire to go up and take a look at God by the works of their own hands. In fact, thousands of church members are hoping to go up into Heaven by the works of their hands, such as church membership, baptism, confirmation, moral living, giving of money, good deeds, etc. But they, too, will find that God has allowed only one way to get to Him and that is through His Son.

In John 14:6, Jesus said, "I am the way. . .no man cometh unto the Father, but by me."

As in the case of Lucifer, so also in this case God stepped in and confused their language and placed a barrier between them that still causes plenty of trouble. I know that every high school student taking Latin and French and every college student wrestling with foreign language study certainly would have appreciated it if these fellows would have let well enough alone.

Now, since men do not learn lessons from God very easily, they are ready again to ascend far above the clouds to make a name for themselves. (See Gen. 11:4.) Will God's pattern hold true this time? Will He send down a judgment on this generation as He did those other two? The Bible promises that, as in every major age or dispensation since the creation of man has ended in judgment, so also shall this present one end.

In the Age of Innocence in the Garden, man was expelled for failure of obedience; the Age of Conscience was brought to a close by the Flood; the Age of Human Government was disrupted by the confusion of tongues over the Tower of Babel; the Age of Promise for Abraham, Isaac and Jacob ended in bondage in Egypt; the Dispensation of Law ended with judgment at the Cross of Calvary. Our present Age of Grace will close with the judgment of the Great Tribulation upon the earth.

But wait. As in Noah's day and in Lot's day, God has promised to spare a remnant. After Noah and his wife, Shem, Ham, and Japheth and their wives were safely into the ark, then the Flood came. In the days of Lot, he and his two daughters were safely out of Sodom when God rained down fire and brimstone out of Heaven.

Luke 17:30 says, "Even thus shall it be in the day when the Son of man is revealed." As God rescued Noah and his family and Lot and his two girls, so shall the Son of God rescue the children of God out of the world before the tribulation sets in under the rule of the Antichrist, who will head up the world church and world government.

Enoch, being translated, and Elijah, being caught up by a whirlwind into Heaven, are Old Testament pictures of the child of God being caught up in the rapture.

I. The Scripture

The great silence of the subject over the land today would lead one to believe that the Bible has very little to say concerning the return of the Lord. Much to the contrary. We find that this is secondary only to the atonement in importance. There are 318 references to it in the New Testament alone.

The first message of the Bible and also the last message deals with the second coming. Notice that Adam, Seth, Enos, Cain, Mahalaleel and Jared never preached, but Enoch, the seventh from Adam, our picture of the rapture in the Old Testament according to Jude 14, prophesied saying, "Behold, the Lord cometh with ten thousand of his saints."

Again notice the last message of the Bible. In Revelation 22:20, just before the benediction of Revelation 22:21, we read, "Even so, come, Lord Jesus."

The Bible is far from silent on this matter.

In Acts 1:11, "Ye men of Galilee, why stand ye gazing up into heaven? This same Jesus, which is taken up from you into heaven, shall so come in like manner as ye have seen him go into heaven."

We read, in John 14:3, "And if I go and prepare a place for you, I will come again. . . ."

First Thessalonians 4:16, 17 says, "For the Lord himself shall descend from heaven with a shout, with the voice of the archangel, and with the trump of God; and the dead in Christ shall rise first: Then we which are alive and remain shall be caught up together with them in the clouds, to meet the Lord in the air: and so shall we ever be with the Lord."

First Corinthians 15:51,52 tells us, "Behold, I shew you a mystery; We shall not all sleep, but we shall all be changed. In a moment, in the twinkling of an eye, at the last trump: for the trumpet shall sound, and the dead shall be raised incorruptible, and we shall be changed."

Second Peter 3:9, 10 says, "The Lord is not slack concerning his promise, as some men count slackness; but is longsuffering to us-ward, not willing that any should perish, but that all should come to repentance. But the day of the Lord will come as a thief in the night. . . ."

Revelation 1:7 states, "Behold, he cometh with clouds; and every eye shall see him. . . ."

Matthew 24:44, "Therefore be ye also ready: for in such an hour as ye think not the Son of man cometh."

The modernist, the infidel and the skeptic might ignore the second coming, but certainly everyone who claims to believe the Bible will have to accept this truth as a major message from the Lord.

II. The Surprise

The sudden, secret appearing of the Lord will be a surprise to the Christian as well as to the unbeliever. No one knows the day or the hour.

The modernist will be surprised. He thought the Bible was old-fashioned and a book for reference, history, etc. The atheist will be surprised. He will find out that he was a fool and that there IS a God. The moralist will be surprised. His good works, church membership, long prayers and social reform program will suddenly be useless.

The drunkard, the harlot, the liar, the thief, the gambler will be surprised because they intended to get things right as soon as they had sowed their wild oats. The movie-goer, the cigarette smoker, the cocktail sipper, the ballroom dancer and the horse race fan will be surprised. They never intended to be caught living that way.

The amillennialist and the postmillennialist will get the surprise of their lives when they discover that they were dead wrong concerning the details of His coming. The group of folks who believe that their church is the only group that is right will be surprised to see members of other denominations that were actually born again! Many Baptists will be shocked to find out that they are not the only ones to be raptured.

The leaders of some of our great denominational programs will have to swallow their pride and blush with shame to realize the independent Bible believers will be accepted by the Lord and caught up to meet Him in the air. The members of cults and isms that have strayed to the teachings of men and women, such as, Mary Baker Eddy, Joseph Russell, Ellen G. White and many others will be surprised. The unsaved man will be surprised when he begins to realize that his small children, wife and good Christian mother have suddenly disappeared.

The procrastinator and neglectful man will be surprised to find out that they didn't have plenty of time, as they thought. The wild, reckless teenager will be surprised to find that the whole lifetime to make up his mind had suddenly been snatched away from him.

The Scripture emphasizes the surprise of the coming of the Lord in many places.

In Matthew, chapter 25, the account of the ten virgins illustrates this. Five were foolish and did not make preparation and were very much surprised by the sudden, unexpected return of the Lord at midnight.

In Matthew 24:27, we read, "For as the lightning cometh out of the east, and shineth even unto the west; so shall also the coming of the Son of man be."

Again, in Revelation 16:15, "Behold, I come as a thief."

In Revelation 3:11, "Behold, I come quickly."

In Revelation 22:20, "Surely, I come quickly."

In Matthew 24:44, we read, "Therefore be ye also ready: for in such as hour as ye think not the Son of man cometh."

Robert Murray McCheyne, the great preacher of the past, once asked a group of folk, "Do you think the Lord will return today?"

One by one they gave their answers, "I think not."

The great man of God then quoted Matthew 24:44, "In such an hour as ye think not the Son of man cometh."

Matthew 25:13 says, "Watch therefore, for ye know neither the day nor the hour wherein the Son of man cometh."

The unsaved person will get another surprise when he finds that it's all over before he realizes it. When the shout is given by the Lord and the trumpet sounds, only the person who has the Holy Spirit living in his heart will recognize the call. To the rest of the world it will be confusing noise.

In Matthew 24:43, the Bible states, ". . .if the goodman of the house had known in what watch the thief would come, he would have watched."

The sudden, secret, soon coming of the Lord will surely be a sorrowful surprise to the majority of the people of the world.

III. Sureness

Jesus said, "I will come again" (John 14:3), but in spite of this clear teaching of the Bible, there are many with the cry, "Where is the promise of his coming?"

Numbers 23:19 says, "God is not a man, that he should lie . . . ."

Again in Romans 3:4, we read, ". . .let God be true, but every man a liar. . . ."

God, Jesus, the Bible and angels testify that He will come again. That ought to settle the matter!

We sing,

> Some golden daybreak, Jesus will come,
>   Some golden daybreak, battles are won.
> He'll shout the victory, break through the blue,
>   Some golden daybreak, for me, for you.

Now, the big question! Friend, do you know that you are prepared for His sudden, secret coming?

Merv Rosell, the well-known evangelist, relates a story of his childhood about the coming of Christ. It seems that his mother, a faithful Christian, had warned him time and time again to get saved lest the Lord should suddenly come and he would be left to go through the tribulation and then, finally end up in the lake of fire. He scoffed at the idea and said, "I'll settle it later."

Then, one day he came home from school and his mother was

not there. He looked all over the house, but no sign of her was to be found. He checked the bedrooms, the cellar, the yard and then, finally he thought, "She's in the prayer closet." Quietly, he opened the door, but bare emptiness stared him in the face. Suddenly his heart jumped into his throat, as he thought, "The Lord has come and I've been left!"

Finally, after he had almost gone into hysterics, the front door opened and in walked his mother.

"Right then and there," relates Mr. Rosell, "I stopped rejecting Christ and received Him as my Saviour. Now I am waiting for His coming instead of fearing it."

Friend, do you fear and dread the thought of His coming? Then, give your heart to Him now and let the thought of His return bring comfort to your heart.

Simple Steps to Spiritual Success

"But thanks be to God, which giveth us the victory through our Lord Jesus Christ."—I Cor. 15:57.

> **Though the sky be dark and drear,**
> **Fierce and strong the gale,**
> **Just remember He is near,**
> **And He will not fail.**

In our text, Paul the apostle is giving testimony to the church at Corinth that in Christ there is victory. It would be well for us to remember, too, that outside of Christ there is no victory, because victory comes as a gift from Christ.

The world seems to have been overcome by Satan and his influence. Satan leaves folks lost, defeated, condemned and in complete failure. Even Christians are defeated, discouraged and failing in their testimony for God because of the power of the Devil. We should remember that God expects us to win and be victorious.

In John 16:33 we read, "These things I have spoken unto you, that in me ye might have peace. In the world ye shall have tribulation: but be of good cheer; I HAVE OVERCOME THE WORLD."

Jesus was never under the circumstances. He was always on top of them. In Revelation 3:21 we are promised, "To him that overcometh will I grant to sit with me in my throne, even as I also overcame, and am set down with my Father in his throne."

First John 5:4 says, "For whosoever is born of God overcometh the world: and this is the victory that overcometh the world, even our faith."

There is no excuse for failure. For the sake of Christ and the Gospel, we must succeed. The Sunday school children sing a little chorus. . .

> **God can do anything, anything, anything.**
> **God can do anything but fail.**
> **He can save, He can keep,**
> **Satisfy with joy complete.**
> **God can do anything but fail.**

First, we must get *victory over sin*. Man has been plagued with sin since Eden. It has dragged him down to the gutter and made him a slave. Man is under bondage to passion, lust, habits and desires of the flesh. He will kill, cheat, lie and steal to satisfy the cravings caused by sin.

Second, we must get *victory over Satan*. First Peter 5:8 tells us, "Be sober, be vigilant; because your adversary the devil, as a roaring lion, walketh about, seeking whom he may devour."

Jesus got the victory over him in the temptations in the wilderness to show that it is possible and to help us know how to do so. The words, "It is written," are the key to success here. We must hide the Word in our heart so that we will not sin against the Lord. Also, by submitting ourselves to the Lord, "he will flee from you" (See James 4:7).

Third, we must get *victory over self*. One great preacher of the past has said, "My greatest enemy is self."

The sin of selfishness bleeds God's work and defeats the spiritual life of the Christian. In Philippians 2:21 we are told, "For all seek their own, not the things which are Jesus Christ's."

Finally, we must get *victory over sorrow*. Many Christians make out well until sickness or death strikes. Then they break. We are to cast our cares and burdens upon the Lord. Our faith and confidence in the will of God is to give us strength. There must be a claiming of the "peace that passeth understanding" (See Phil. 4:7). Paul states, "For I have learned, in whatsoever state I am, therewith to be content."

Again he says, in Philippians 4:4, "Rejoice in the Lord alway: and again I say, Rejoice."

We must remember, too, that "all things work together for good to them that love God" (Rom. 8:28).

I. Control of the Spirit

There is no spiritual success without the leadership of the Holy Spirit. When Christ left earth for Heaven, He promised to send the One who would convict, teach, comfort and lead us for the Lord. The Holy Spirit came down upon the believers at Pentecost and they spake with tongues. He then began to work through believers to speak to sinners.

In John 16:8 we are told, "And when he is come, he will reprove the world of sin, and of righteousness, and of judgment."

Now, the Holy Spirit points out, or acquaints a person with the fact that he is a sinner. He then reveals the righteousness of Christ and Calvary; then He announces and reminds that judgment must come. The Spirit speaks through the Word of God and brings conviction. If the heart's door is opened and Christ is invited in, this gives salvation.

First we see the *incoming of the Spirit*. There is an empty spot in the heart of man for the Holy Spirit, put there by God. Amusements, thrills, sports and busy schedules will not fill this spot. In Revelation 3:20 He promises, "If any man hear my voice, and open the door, I will come in to him, and will sup with him, and he with me."

When the door of the heart is opened by the sinner, the Spirit of God enters and is born into his heart. This is why Jesus told Nicodemus, in John 3:7, "Ye must be born again."

> **Into my heart, into my heart,**
> **Come into my heart, Lord Jesus.**
> **Come in today, come in to stay,**
> **Come into my heart, Lord Jesus.**

Second, notice the *indwelling of the Spirit*. First Corinthians 3:16 says, "Know ye not that ye are the temple of God, and that the Spirit of God dwelleth in you?"

First John 2:27 tells us, "But the anointing which ye have received of him abideth in you. . . ."

James 4:5 speaks of, "The spirit that dwelleth in us. . . ."

John 14:17 tells of, "Even the Spirit of truth. . .dwelleth with you, and shall be in you."

Through the indwelling Holy Spirit, we have communion with God and He gives us comfort, courage and instruction. God is as near as our hearts.

Third, see the *infilling of the Spirit*. Ephesians 5:18 exhorts us, "But be filled with the Spirit."

The word "filled" here speaks of saturation. We are to be submitted to His will and empty of self. When we are empty, He will fill us with instruction of what to do, give us power to do it, and give a blessing because we do.

The majority of Christians know nothing of the filling of the Spirit; yet, Ephesians 5:18 is a clear command of God. Therefore, it is direct disobedience and a sin not to seek, yield and submit for the filling of the Holy Spirit.

Finally, notice the *instruction of the Spirit*. Victory and power depend upon being in the will of God. Jesus said that when the Spirit is come He will teach you all things. He will help you to know what to do and how to do it. He will also help you to know what *not* to do.

If you want spiritual success, you must first be controlled by the Spirit. Let me illustrate. When I drive my car, I must be in full control. When I need to stop I apply the brakes. At night when the lights are needed, I decide when to turn them on. When I want to turn left, the car must obey and turn left. Now, think what a mess we would have if the car decided to make its own decisions and be in full control itself. When a child runs across the road and I hit the brakes, suppose the car does not want to stop. Or, suppose when I decided to turn left, the car decided to go straight. I wouldn't have a car like that!

When I need a horn, I want a horn; when I need brakes, I want brakes and when I want to stop or turn left, speed up or go backward, I want the car to be in full sympathy with me.

Now, in the spiritual life, we are the car and the Holy Spirit is the driver. How foolish of us not to allow Him full control.

II. Confession of Salvation and Sins

The second step to spiritual success is confession. There must, first of all, be a daily *confession of our Saviour.* We are told to confess with our mouth that which we believe in our heart (See Rom. 10:9).

In Matthew 10:32, Jesus said, "Whosoever therefore shall confess me before men, him will I confess also before my Father which is in heaven."

Again, in I John 4:15, we read, "Whosoever shall confess that Jesus is the Son of God, God dwelleth in him, and he in God."

Every newborn child of God should make public confession in church and before all the world that he has accepted Christ as personal Saviour. Then, from that time on, there should be daily confession with the mouth and with the life in order that the life might speak for Christ. We are the salt of the earth and our job as Christians is to make the world thirsty for the Water of Life.

In Philippians 2:11, Paul declares, "And that every tongue should confess that Jesus Christ is Lord, to the glory of God the Father."

Peter was asked by Jesus, in Matthew 16:15, "But whom say ye that I am?"

And Peter passed with flying colors when he stated, "Thou art the Christ, the Son of the living God" (Matt. 16:16).

Thomas doubted and refused to accept the testimony of the eleven until he had placed his hand in the wounds of Jesus; but, after this, he confessed, "My Lord and my God" (John 20:28).

When Philip read about Christ from Isaiah, the Ethiopian eunuch wanted to be baptized. Philip asked him if he believed with all his heart. The eunuch confessed, "I believe that Jesus Christ is the Son of God" (Acts 8:37).

On one occasion, Peter denied the Lord three times and refused to confess Him. The result speaks for itself. Peter went out and wept bitterly (See Luke 22:62).

Second, we are to *confess our sins.* Proverbs 28:13 states, "He that covereth his sins shall not prosper; but whoso confesseth and forsaketh them shall have mercy."

We are promised in I John 1:9, "If we confess our sins, he is faithful and just to forgive us our sins, and to cleanse us from all unrighteousness."

Ezra declares, in Ezra 10:11, "Now therefore make confession unto the Lord God of your fathers. . . ."

In the Old Testament account of the battle of Ai, Achan stole gold and silver. The blessings of God were taken away from Israel. Joshua cried out to God and God told Joshua to clean the sin out of the camp. Achan was found out. In Joshua 7:20, we read of Achan's confession of sins: "And Achan answered Joshua, and said, Indeed I have sinned against the Lord God of Israel, and thus and thus have I done."

Achan gave a factual account of his sin. This is the pattern of true confession.

Elsewhere in the Bible men have confessed their sins, after they were caught. Balaam came to his senses and confessed to the angel, "I have sinned; for I knew not. . ." (Num. 22:34).

Samuel heard the bleating of the sheep behind Saul's barn and exposed the sin of Saul's disobedience. First Samuel 15:24,25 records Saul's confession: "I have sinned; for I have transgressed the commandment of the Lord, and thy words: because I feared the people, and obeyed their voice. Now therefore, I pray thee, pardon my sin, and turn again with me, that I may worship the Lord."

Nathan pointed his accusing finger in David's face and said, "Thou art the man" (II Sam. 12:7).

David confessed, "I have sinned against the Lord" (II Sam. 12:13).

After Peter saw Jesus walking on the water, he realized his need to confess sins. He said to the Lord, "Depart from me; for I am a sinful man, O Lord" (Luke 5:8).

The prodigal son came to the end of the road and, in the filth and smell of the hogpen, he realized that confession was his only way out. Thank God, he wasn't too proud to confess, "I have sinned against heaven. . ." (Luke 15:18).

For victory and success, we must learn that confession of our daily sins is of major importance.

III. Compassion for Souls

Being controlled by the Spirit will give us power to overcome, while confession will give us cleansing. Now, a compassion for souls will give us energy and drive to fulfill the Great Commission.

The main work of the church is winning the lost. All our activities, such as, church papers, radio broadcasts, the buses, the building, the Bible clubs, the missionary program, Sunday school, advertisements and revival campaigns and all the rest are to help us win more souls to Christ. If the motive is not right, the work will not count for Christ.

Jesus had a compassion for souls. On many occasions the Bible says that He had compassion for the multitudes. When He saw a blind man, He gave sight. When He saw a cripple, He healed him. His compassion bid Him to work many miracles. These people, in turn, believed on Him as Saviour and Lord. Jesus wept over Jerusalem.

Paul was driven by a holy unrest in his soul for the lost. Livingstone and such men caught some of this and set the world on fire for Jesus. Fill your churches with bankers, lawyers, scientists, educators and men of importance, culture and knowledge, but I will choose a church full of folks who have a driving passion for souls. Means and methods are worthless without a right motivation.

Remember, Jesus came to "seek and to save that which was lost" (Luke 19:10).

Any man who will be close to the heart of God will need to be concerned about the same things that God is concerned about.

There are many formulas for success but, dear reader, if you can please the Lord and be a victorious, happy Christian, be controlled by the Holy Spirit, confess Christ and sins daily and have a compassion for souls, then you will have what you are looking for in this life and will look back from eternity with gratitude for God's blessing.